Many Things
Most Christians
Do Not Know

Rev. Lloyd E. Stinnett D.D.

outskirts
press

Acknowledgements

This is a list of all who made this book possible, in alphabetical order by last name, except for the most important name of all. Thank you, love you, and could not have accomplished it without your help.

Jesus Christ
Pastor Keith Cameron
Grant Croley
Patty Curtis
Lonnie Dillard
Rose Hayden
Rev. Teddy House
Wilborn House
Robert Kidd (EditFast.com)
Arlon Benton Stinnett
Virginia L. Stinnett

Table of Contents

Foreword

I know I put myself out there with the title of this book. Do I really know what I am talking about, or just making it up to sell a book? The contents of this book will give Theologians something to argue about for years…or not. I truly believe I was inspired by God to write this book, cause I just ain't that smart on me own. LOL. I wrote this book for four different reasons.

1. To inspire Christians and make them more knowledgeable of what is going on in this day, and time. Also, to help them re-establish their faith much stronger than ever before so you will pray more, read the Bible more, witness and invite others to church, and find ways to participate more in their church.
2. To encourage those who have fallen away from the faith and get them back to a Bible based church and turn their life back over to a Savior risen-from-the grave, named Jesus.
3. To help those doubters out there to know that what the Bible says is true and inspired by the Holy Spirit.
4. To help those who are lost come to the salvation, love, and forgiveness of the only true living God.

There is much scripture to prove what is said here in this book. I did it that way so you are not just reading what Lloyd is saying to you, but what the Lord is saying to you. Many people who do write books, tell of their accomplishments, and that is good. But for me, I cannot do that. Earlier in my life, I was probably one of the most sinful, wretched, wicked persons out there. It is something I shamefully admit. But since becoming a Christian, anything I may have accomplished, including this book, I have to give my God all the credit. For all those that I have done wrong in the past, I deeply regret what I have done, and hope you can find it in your heart to forgive me, and in doing so, turn your life over to Jesus, so I can apologize to each and every one of you in Heaven. In the true stories I tell you here, you will notice I do not mention names, places, or dates. They are not needed to make the points I want to make, plus, I am not out to embarrass anyone.

Early on, in my ministry, I learned four things.

1. It is not about me.
2. Never was about me.
3. Never will be about me.
4. It is all about Jesus.

All the good and positive things that happen because of this book, I give all the credit to God, and only God. On the opposite side of the coin, I will take all the blame.

With Love In Christ!

Rev. Lloyd E. Stinnett D. D.

P.S. For those who do not know. The different initials I use to reference the Bible, are different versions of that scripture (NIV New International Version, or KJV: King James Version). Most of the time, my usage is because it is easier to understand, and other times, because I feel it explains it better.

Tick Tock Says the Clock

The clock below says twelve midnight and that it may be too late, but is it really? Not quite, but the time is getting very, very close folks, before the return of Jesus. So, do not wait until this clock says it is too late.

If you look at your clock folks, is it still running?

That maybe so, but God's eternal clock, in regards to that as the last minutes before the Rapture, will someday happen, and will happen soon.

If midnight on God's clock, was the time of the rapture,
I can see the time almost at hand.

Will you be taken?

Or will you be left behind?

You now have the most important decision of your life to make!

Will you be taken in the Rapture? Or will you be left behind? You now have the most important decision of your life to make!

Who Is God?

Who is God? What do we know about Him? Do the scriptures give us any insight? Yes! God has so many attributes, I will not try to list them all. Here are just a few:

All powerful. Even Satan, who was close to God, thought he knew everything about God, and Heaven. Ezekiel 28:12-16 NIV: (Talking about Satan.) "Son of man, take up a lament concerning the king of Tyre and say to him: 'This is what the Sovereign LORD says: 'You were the seal of perfection, full of wisdom and perfect in beauty. You were in Eden, the garden of God; every precious stone adorned you: carnelian, chrysolite and emerald, topaz, onyx and jasper, lapis lazuli, turquoise and beryl. Your settings and mountings were made of gold; on the day you were created they were prepared. You were anointed as a guardian cherub, for so I ordained you. You were on the holy mount of God; you walked among the fiery stones. You were blameless in your ways from the day you were created till wickedness was found in you. Through your widespread trade you were filled with violence, and you sinned. So, I drove you in disgrace from the mount of God, and I expelled you, guardian cherub, from among the fiery stones.'"

Satan did not realize how powerful God was until: Luke 10:18 NIV: (Jesus talking) He replied, "I saw Satan fall like lightning from heaven." After the devil betrayed God, he found out how powerful He really is.

All knowing. 1 John 3:20 NIV: "If our hearts condemn us, we know that God is greater than our hearts, and He knows everything."

Merciful. John 3:16 NIV: "For God so loved the world that He gave His one and only Son, that whoever believes in Him shall not perish but have eternal life."

Loving. 1 John 4:8 NIV: "Whoever does not love does not know God, because God is love."

Caring. Matthew 10:29-31 NIV: "Are not two sparrows sold for a penny? Yet not one of them will fall to the ground outside your Father's care. And even the very hairs of your head are all numbered. So don't be afraid; you are worth more than many sparrows."

Forgiving. 1 John 1:9 NIV: "If we confess our sins, He is faithful and just and will forgive us our sins and purify us from all unrighteousness."

Full of grace. Psalm 45:8 NIV: "The Lord is gracious and compassionate, slow to anger and rich in love."

Omnipotent. Webster's dictionary says Omnipotent is:

1. Almighty
2. having virtually unlimited authority or influence
3. an omnipotent ruler

Scripture says: Nehemiah 9:6 NIV: "You alone are the LORD. You made the heavens, even the highest heavens, and all their starry hosts, the earth and all that is on it, the seas and all that is in them. You give life to everything, and the multitudes of heaven worship You."

Omnipresent. Webster's dictionary says Omnipresent is: present in all places at all times. Scripture says: Jeremiah 23:24 KJV "Can any hide himself in secret places that I shall not see him? saith the LORD.

Do not I fill heaven and earth? saith the LORD."

His ways are not our ways. Scripture: Isaiah 55:8 NIV: "For My thoughts are not your thoughts, neither are your ways My ways," declares the Lord. Do not try to second guess God. What a great, and awesome, God we serve!

Black and White VS Interpretation

Before we get into the book itself, I would like to help those who are having trouble understanding the Bible. First of all, if understanding the Bible is a problem for you, find yourself a simpler version to understand, such a NIV: (New International Version), ESV (English Standard Version), or a version that may not be as hard to comprehend, as the KJV (King James Version) is difficult for many. If you are a new Christian or finding it difficult to understand the Bible, please stay away from the Amplified Bible. The simplification they use may be harder for you to understand than the King James Version.

"Black And White" in what you read, clearly means what it says.

Definition of the word 'Interpretation': The act or result of explaining or interpreting something or the way something is explained or understood.

It is much easier to read the Bible when you break it down to either 'Black Or White', or 'Interpretation'. For example, if you read:

John 6:19 NIV: "When they had rowed about three or four miles, they saw Jesus approaching the boat, walking on the water; and they were frightened."

That is black and white, in other words, it actually happened, so what it said, is what is meant. Now I have a trick question for you. When you read: Matthew 13:3-9 NIV: (Jesus talking.) "Then He told them many things in parables, saying: 'A farmer went out to sow his seeds. As he was scattering the seeds, some fell along the path, and the birds came and ate them up. Some fell on rocky places, where they did not have much soil. They sprang up quickly, because the soil was shallow. But when the sun came up, the plants were scorched, and they withered because they had no root. Other seeds fell among thorns, which grew up and choked the plants. Still other seeds fell on good soil, where they produced a crop—a hundred, sixty or thirty times what was sown. Whoever has ears, let them hear.'"

Is that black and white, or interpretation? Now remember, I said it was a trick question. At that point, it was interpretation, but when Jesus explained it, in the scripture below, it becomes black and white. Matthew 13:18– 23 NIV: (Jesus talking.) "Listen then to what the parable of the sower means: When anyone hears the message about the kingdom and does not understand it, the evil one comes and snatches away what was sown in their heart. This is the seed sown along the path. The seed falling on rocky ground refers to someone who hears the word and at once receives it with joy. But since they have no root, they last only a short time. When trouble or persecution comes because of the word, they quickly fall away. The seed falling among the thorns refers to someone who hears the word, but the worries of this life and the deceitfulness of wealth choke the word, making it unfruitful. But the seed falling on good soil refers to someone who hears the word and understands it. This is the one who produces a crop, yielding a hundred, sixty, or thirty times what was sown."

This is why we have so many denominations. So many have trouble in their interpretation of the Bible. Crazy as it may seem, some people/ religions take a scripture that is black and white and try to interpret it.

With that in mind, the scripture below is not saying that He, Jesus, is the Father, but everything the Father says, and does, is identical to what He (Jesus) believes. Please read the second scripture. In the next chapter I will show you that the Father, Son, and Holy Spirit, are three different persons, together called the "Trinity"

John 14:9 KJV: "Jesus saith unto him, Have I been so long time with you, and yet hast thou not known Me, Philip? He that hath seen Me hath seen the Father; and how sayest thou then, 'Shew us the Father'?"

John 12:49 KJV: (Jesus speaking) "For I have not spoken of Myself; but the Father which sent Me, He gave Me a commandment, what I should say, and what I should speak."

See, He says in the last scripture, that He is not the Father. I will further explain this in the next chapter.

Trinity

The word "Trinity" is confusing. Is it three separate beings (Father, Son, and Holy Spirit), or is it one being as some religions seem to believe? The Bible gives us the answer to that so many times, and the answer is quite simple.

From Wikipedia, the word "Trinity" means: The Christian doctrine of the Trinity (Latin: *Trinitas*, lit. "triad", from Greek τριάς and τριάδα, from Latin: *trinus* "threefold") holds that God is not one but three coeternal, consubstantial persons or hypostases—the Father, the Son (Jesus Christ), and the Holy Spirit—as "one God in three Divine Persons." The three Persons are distinct, yet are one "substance, essence, or nature" (homoousios). In this context, a "nature" is *what* one is, whereas a "person" is *who* one is. Sometimes differing views are referred to as nontrinitarian.

According to this central mystery of most Christian faiths, there is only one God in three Persons: while distinct in their relations with each other ("It is the Father who generates, the Son who is begotten, and the Holy Spirit who proceeds"), they are stated to be one in all else, co-equal, co-eternal, consubstantial, and each is God, whole and entire. Accordingly, the whole work of creation and grace in Christianity, is seen as a single operation, common to all three divine persons in which each shows forth what is proper to him in the Trinity, so that all things are *from* the Father, *through* the Son and *in* the Holy Spirit.

Now that I got that out of the way, let's see what the Bible says. There are many scriptures that answer this question, but I plan to hit a just a few of the major ones.

Genesis 1:26 NIV: "Then God said, 'Let us make mankind in Our image, in Our likeness, so that they may rule over the fish in the sea, and the birds in the sky, over the livestock and all the wild animals, and over all the creatures that move along the ground.'"

Did you notice the word "Our"?

Matthew 3-17 NIV: "And a voice from heaven said, 'This is My Son, whom I love; with Him I am well pleased.'"

This is the Father speaking. Is He speaking of Himself? Of course not. If He did, He would say: "with *Me* I am well pleased." That sounds stupid, doesn't it? Our God is neither a stupid, nor an arrogant God.

Matthew 26-39 NIV: (Jesus speaking.) "Going a little farther, He fell with His face to the ground and prayed, 'My Father, if it is possible, may this cup be taken from Me. Yet not as I will, but as Your will.'"

In return, this is Jesus talking to the Father. Had Jesus, and the Father, been the same person, why would He even say this?

Luke 23:34 NIV: "Jesus said, 'Father, forgive them, for they do not know what they are doing.' And they divided up His clothes by casting lots." Once again Jesus is talking to the Father.

Matthew 28:19 NIV: "Therefore, go and make disciples of all nations, baptizing them in the name of the Father, and of the Son, and of the Holy Spirit." This is Jesus speaking. Even He separates the three, as three different persons.

MARK 16:19 NIV: "He was taken up to Heaven and sat down at the right hand of God." (The Father.)

So, do you truly believe if He was just one Person that He would be sitting at the right hand of...Himself? Of course not. I am sure you have figured it all out by now. I could write pages, upon pages, on this subject, but I guess you are wondering why I have not said anything about the Holy Spirit. Well here goes.

John 16:7-8 NIV: (Jesus speaking): "But very truly I tell you, it is for your good that I am going away. Unless I go away, the Advocate will not come to you; but if I go, I will send Him to you. When He comes, He will prove the world to be in the wrong about sin and righteousness and judgment."

John 14:16 NIV: (Jesus speaking) "And I will ask the Father, and He will give you another Advocate to help you and be with you forever."

Dictionary.com says "Another" means: "a different one", or another meaning is: "a person other than oneself.

This of course, is the Holy Spirit, the third member of the Trinity. So, presently Jesus is in heaven, and will not come back, until His second coming, and then His thousand-year reign here on earth.

So, when is Jesus coming back? No one on earth really knows just as the scripture says:

Mark 13:32 NIV: (Jesus speaking) "But about that day or hour no one knows, not even the angels in heaven, nor the Son, but only the Father.

Once again, this scripture proves that Jesus, and the Father, are two different Beings.

Matthew 24:30 NIV: (Jesus speaking) "Then will appear the sign of the Son of Man in heaven. And then all the peoples of the earth will mourn when they see the Son of Man coming on the clouds of heaven, with power and great glory."

We like to call it the "Rapture", but whatever you may want to call it, how glorious a day it will be for those who are saved. If you are not, I will give you a chance at the end of the book, or you can just jump there right now.

Trinity Three as One

Now, my challenge to you is to find as many scriptures as you can, proving that the Father, Son (Jesus), and the Holy Spirit are three different persons. I promise you, there are so many out there, it almost bogles the mind. How is that even possible? We talked, and hopefully proved, that there are three, as one, we call the "Trinity". Does it really show in the Bible how that can be? I believe God has showed and proved it to me. But don't the first four of God's Commandments contradict what I have been saying? Not at all, once you hear you will know—as Paul Harvey used to say—"The rest of the story." And there is scripture to prove it. But don't the scriptures below prove there is only one God (Person.)?

Exodus 20:2-7:

1. "I am the LORD your God, who brought you out of the land of Egypt, out of the house of slavery."
2. "You shall have no other gods before Me."
3. "You shall not make for yourself an idol, or any likeness of what is in heaven above or on the earth beneath or in the water under the earth. You shall not worship them or serve them; for I, the LORD your God, am a jealous God, visiting the iniquity of the fathers on the children, on the third and the

fourth generations of those who hate Me, but showing loving kindness to thousands, to those who love Me and keep My commandments."

4. "You shall not take the name of the LORD your God in vain, for the LORD will not leave him unpunished who takes His name in vain."

After reading that, let me explain how God showed me how all this works.

Genesis 2:24 NIV: "That is why a man leaves his father and mother and is united to his wife, and they become one flesh."

But it is much more than just flesh only.

Ephesians 5:23 NIV: "For the husband is the head of the wife as Christ is the head of the church, His body, of which He is the Savior."

Just as a man and wife become as one in marriage. The Father, Son, and Holy Spirit have also been united as one, in a spiritual marriage which we will be part of in the very near future.

Marriage of the Lamb

Revelations 19:6-10 NIV: "Then I heard what sounded like a great multitude, like the roar of rushing waters and like loud peals of thunder, shouting: 'Hallelujah! For our Lord God Almighty reigns. Let us rejoice and be glad and give Him glory! For the wedding of the Lamb has come, and His bride has made herself ready. Fine linen, bright and clean, was given her to wear.' (Fine linen stands for the righteous acts of God's holy people.) Then the angel said to me, 'Write this: Blessed are those who are invited to the wedding supper of the Lamb!' And he added, 'These are the true words of God.' At this I fell at his feet to worship him. But he said to me, 'Don't do that! I am a fellow servant with you, and with your brothers and sisters who hold to the testimony of Jesus. Worship God! For it is the Spirit of prophecy who bears testimony to Jesus.'"

This is a marriage in the Spiritual sense. We are grafted into that marriage of the Trinity: The Father, the Son (Jesus), and the Holy Spirit. In that order. The Father is the head of the Trinity. Do I have proof for that? I sure do. First of all, remember Mark 13:32 we previously talked about where even Jesus said He does not know the time of His second coming, but the Father only in Heaven knows.

Romans 8:34 V.I.V. Who then is the one who condemns? No one. Christ Jesus who died and who was raised to life, is at the right hand of God and is also interceding for us.

Matthew 20:20-21 NIV: "Then the mother of Zebedee's sons came to Jesus with her sons and, kneeling down, asked a favor of Him. 'What is it you want?' He asked. She said, 'Grant that one of these two sons of mine may sit at Your right and the other at Your left in Your kingdom.'"

Although she asked Jesus to let two of His disciples sit at the right, and left of Him in Heaven, His reply was:

Matthew 20:23 NIV: "Jesus said to them, 'You will indeed drink from My cup, but to sit at My right or left is not for Me to grant. These places belong to those for whom they have been prepared by My Father.'"

So, as I said before, The Father is the head of the Trinity. As Christians, we must not forget this.

1 John 2:1 NIV: "My dear children, I write this to you so that you will not sin. But if anybody does sin, we have an advocate with the Father through Jesus Christ, the Righteous One."

There are other scriptures to prove this, but I hope this is enough to persuade you. Are you convinced of this? I sure am and I hope and pray that you can see it too.

G. D. WORDS

As a Christian minister, I hate to hear those dreaded four letter words. Of course the two I particularly hate the worst is: First of all, the "G.D." word we here so frequently, and the "N" word. With all the profanity in this world, whether it be movies, television, music, on the internet, in writing, books, out of people's mouth, and even young children, and the list goes on. I thought it would be nice, for us, to have our own 'G.D.', and 'N' words. Here are some I came up with. Can you think of some of your own?

1. GOD DESERVES
2. GOD DEMANDS
3. GOD DELIVERS
4. GOD DECIDES
5. GOD DECLARES
6. GOD DEFEATS
7. GOD DEFENDS
8. GOD DELIGHTS
9. GOD'S DESIGN
10. GOD DESIRES
11. GOD DIRECTS
12. GOD DISCIPLINES

13. GOD DOES
14. GOD DIVIDES

Maybe some of the "n" words we could use instead are:

1. Nicest
2. Neighborly
3. Noble

The best one I could come up with, but without the "N' is: I love you my Christian Black Brothers and Sisters in Christ.

DNA & Genetics

Deoxyribonucleic Acid, also known as DNA, is most commonly discussed in a section of science called "Biochemistry".

The English Oxford Dictionary describes DNA like this: "Deoxyribonucleic acid, a self-replicating material which is present in nearly all living organisms as the main constituent of chromosomes. It is the carrier of genetic information. Each molecule of DNA consists of two strands coiled round each other to form a double helix, a structure like a spiral ladder. Each rung of the ladder consists of a pair of chemical groups called bases (of which there are four types), which combine in specific pairs so that the sequence on one strand of the double helix is complementary to that on the other: it is the specific sequence of bases which constitutes the genetic information."

Well, not sure I really understand it all, but I do understand this. We are all together on this world. There are so many prejudices that should not exist that it just blows my mind. But why? At the end of this chapter I will prove we are all related through D. N.A. As God says in Acts 10:34-35 KJV: "Then Peter opened his mouth, and said, Of a truth I perceive that God is no respecter of persons: But in every nation he that feareth Him, and worketh righteousness, is accepted with Him."

John 3:14-19 NIV: "Just as Moses lifted up the snake in the

wilderness, so the Son of Man must be lifted up, that everyone who believes may have eternal life in Him. For God so loved the world that He gave His one and only Son, that whoever believes in Him shall not perish but have eternal life. For God did not send His Son into the world to condemn the world, but to save the world through Him. Whoever believes in Him is not condemned, but whoever does not believe stands condemned already because they have not believed in the name of God's one and only Son. This is the verdict: Light has come into the world, but people loved darkness instead of light because their deeds were evil."

There is so much Scripture in which God does not see the prejudices. Then are we better than a sovereign God?

Years ago, early in my ministry, I was asked by a black pastor friend of mine, to sing at his church, on a Monday for Rev. Martin Luther King's birthday service. So, I actually went to his church to hear him preach the Sunday before, and I talked to him before the service that morning. He did a fine job, and actually sang his sermon. Through his service though, he kept talking about 'Whitey and the dogs'. Being in a church with over 100 blacks, and one white (me), I began to worry about what I should do. Thinking of trying to find a way out, I found the windows were closed, ushers at the doors, and me in the middle of the congregation. So, I stayed. It turned out to be one of the friendliest churches I have ever been to. I wondered if maybe they just felt sorry for me, or thought I was just that brave. I seriously believe, even after all that the pastor said, they were just a good, loving, Christian Church. In fact, they even asked me to sing there again. Did I say something to my pastor friend? No. Maybe I should have, but I was new in the ministry about 28 years ago and did not really know how to approach him on this. On what I showed you of what God said, we as Christians should find ways to unite in denominations of Bible-based churches, races, nationalities, and not divide. Please, by the Grace of God, let's keep all these prejudices out of our churches, and find ways to show love to our fellow Brothers and Sisters in Christ.

So many people are taught prejudices at such an early age. They were taught, that they were superior to certain races, nationalities, people, or that others were inferior, and so much more. On the flip side, many are taught they are of low class or whatever and believe they are inferior. Unfortunately, many will go through their whole life believing they are inferior. Trust me, these teachings are not in the Bible. These are the teachings of a misguided and fearful mankind, which is contrary to what the Bible teaches us. For example, if everyone tells a child, who is a genius, that he is an idiot, his confidence will not grow and when older, he will probably believe he is an idiot and never accomplish the great things he could have done in life. I know of those who, as a child, were told by their fathers that they will never make anything of themselves in life, and that resonated in their mind through adulthood. All these, and more types of prejudices must stop because, I promise you, they will...when Jesus returns.

I wanted to save this for last. Years ago, I was watching a documentary on an educational program and I heard something I thought was very profound. There were two men, who went around the world taking samples of the D.N.A. of every tribe, nation, and race. First of all, let me say that they never said anything about God, Jesus, the Bible, or any form of religion. Also, if I remember right, there was a little cussing in it. Although I did not find it very interesting, I wanted to find out the outcome, and I am glad I did. The two conclusions were:

1. That everyone comes from one woman, and as Christians we know her as Eve. Genesis 3:20 NIV: "Adam named his wife Eve, because she would become the mother of all the living."

2. Their second conclusion was that she was from China. Now this I do not know. But Adam and Eve were thrown out of the Garden of Eden for defying God, and were deceived by the devil.

Genesis 3:2-5 NIV: "The woman said to the serpent, 'We may eat fruit from the trees in the garden, but God did say, 'You must not eat fruit from the tree that is in the middle of the garden, and you must not touch it, or you will die.'"

"You will not certainly die," the serpent said to the woman. "For God knows that when you eat from it your eyes will be opened, and you will be like God, knowing good and evil."

Although man may think they know where the Garden of Eden is, I have my doubts.

Genesis: 3:24 NIV: "After He drove the man out, He placed on the east side of the Garden of Eden cherubim and a flaming sword flashing back and forth to guard the way to the tree of life."

Although we have places on earth that are very beautiful, I am not sure I know of any place, on Earth, that I would call a Garden of Eden. Besides, I imagine that angel is still guarding it, to keep us out, for all of our sins. But it's your call!

The Salvation Plan

Which denomination gets me to Heaven? Guess what, no denomination will get you to Heaven. You can even go to Church every time the doors open, and that will not do it. Some denominations want you to think that, if you do not go to their Church, you will not go to Heaven. Wrong! Some of them, I believe, just say that so as not to lose members. So, you may think, *I am a good person and that will be enough.* Wrong again!

Psalm 53:3 NIV: "Everyone has turned away, all have become corrupt; there is no one who does good, not even one."

Isaiah 64:6 NIV: "All of us have become like one who is unclean, and all our righteous acts are like filthy rags; we all shrivel up like a leaf, and like the wind our sins sweep us away."

Luke 18:19 NIV: "Why do you call Me good? Jesus answered. No one is good—except God alone."

So, how do we get to Heaven and be forgiven?

Romans 10:9-13 NIV: "If you declare with your mouth, 'Jesus is Lord,' and believe in your heart that God raised Him from the dead, you will be saved. For it is with your heart that you believe and are justified, and it is with your mouth that you profess your faith and are saved." As Scripture says, Romans 10:11 NIV: "Anyone who believes in Him will never be put to shame. For there is no difference between

Jew and Gentile—the same Lord is Lord of all and richly blesses all who call on Him, for, Everyone who calls on the name of the Lord will be saved."

So, it is in the heart. Getting your heart right with God. You see, God wants everyone to go to Heaven, but He gave us a free will to make that choice. He did not want a bunch of puppets here on earth, or in Heaven, but those who truly love, worship, serve, and want to follow Him. I am sure you have heard this many times, but have you listened to the scriptures to go along with it?

John 3:15-18 NIV: "That everyone who believes may have eternal life in Him. For God so loved the world that He gave His one and only Son, that whoever believes in Him shall not perish but have eternal life. For God did not send His Son into the world to condemn the world, but to save the world through Him. Whoever believes in Him is not condemned, but whoever does not believe stands condemned already because they have not believed in the name of God's one and only Son."

So, it is by faith, love, worship, and forgiveness that we can attain God's mercy and grace. In the end, it is really your call. Do you really want Jesus, in your lives? Do you really wish to go to Heaven? Your only other alternative is:

Romans 6:23 NIV: "For the wages of sin is death, but the gift of God is eternal life in Christ Jesus our Lord."

Revelations 20:15 NIV: "Anyone whose name was not found written in the book of life was thrown into the lake of fire."

John 3:36 NIV: "Whoever believes in the Son has eternal life, but whoever rejects the Son will not see life, for God's wrath remains on them."

Colossians 3:1-2 NIV: "Since, then, you have been raised with Christ, set your hearts on things above, where Christ is, seated at the right hand of God. Set your minds on things above, not on earthly things."

Colossians 3:23-24 NIV: "Whatever you do, work at it with all your heart, as working for the Lord, not for human masters, since you know that you will receive an inheritance from the Lord as a reward. It is the Lord Christ you are serving."

Proverbs 4:23 NIV: "Above all else, guard your heart, for everything you do flows from it."

In other words, if what people are telling you does not align with the Bible, do not get involved with their way of thinking. There are a lot of foolish ideas and theories out there now. In fact, some have ideas about what the Bible says, means, or should mean that are very outlandish. My hope is that, in reading this book, your heart will be right, and always be right with God.

All this, is for those who are going to a real place called "HELL" for eternity, and that means forever. This is a place no one should desire to ever want to be.

Dictionary.com describes Hell as: "The place or state of punishment of the wicked after death; the abode of evil and condemned spirits; any place or state of torment or misery: something that causes torment or misery.

The Free Dictionary on the internet describes Eternity as:

1. Time without beginning or end; infinite time.
2. The state or quality of being eternal.
3. The timeless state following death

Definitely does not sound like a good place to be for even one second let alone forever. You have the free will (choice) and the decision on where you would want to be when you pass on is yours. To me it's a no brainer. Think very seriously about this before you make the wrong choice. It's your decision to make! Please do not make the wrong one!

The Beatitudes of Jesus

Matthew 5:1–12 KJV

Blessed are the poor in spirit: for theirs is the kingdom of heaven.
Blessed are they that mourn: for they shall be comforted.
Blessed are the meek: for they shall inherit the earth.
Blessed are they which do hunger and thirst after righteousness:
for they shall be filled.
Blessed are the merciful: for they shall obtain mercy.
Blessed are the pure in heart: for they shall see God.
Blessed are the peacemakers: for they shall be called the
children of God.
Blessed are they who are persecuted for righteousness' sake: for theirs is the
kingdom of heaven.
Blessed are ye, when men shall revile you, and persecute you, and shall say
all manner of evil against you falsely, for My sake.

Doubts

Are you one of those doubters? The devil will do that to you. But maybe this chapter will give you a gleam of hope. Remember how John the Baptist knew who Jesus was?

John 1:26–27 NIV: "I baptize with water," John replied, "but among you stands One you do not know. He is the One Who comes after me, the straps of whose sandals I am not worthy to untie."

Matthew 3:13–17 NIV: "Then Jesus came from Galilee to the Jordan to be baptized by John. But John tried to deter Him, saying, "I need to be baptized by You, and do You come to me?" Jesus replied, "Let it be so now; it is proper for us to do this to fulfill all righteousness." Then John consented. As soon as Jesus was baptized, He went up out of the water. At that moment heaven was opened, and He saw the Spirit of God descending like a dove and alighting on Him. And a voice from heaven said, "This is my Son, whom I love; with Him I am well pleased."

But later, with the difficulties of his life, while in prison, even John had his doubts.

John 7:20– 22 NIV: "When the men came to Jesus, they said, 'John the Baptist sent us to you to ask, 'Are You the One Who is to come, or should we expect someone else?' At that very time Jesus cured many who had diseases, sicknesses and evil spirits, and gave sight to many who were blind. So He replied to the messengers, 'Go back and report to John what you have seen and heard: The blind receive sight, the lame walk, those who have leprosy are cleansed, the deaf hear, the dead are raised, and the good news is proclaimed to the poor."

But I can honestly tell you there is much hope in Jesus Christ. But why then, when I am struggling, does it take so long to get my prayers answered? As you know sometimes the answer is 'Yes', other times 'No', and in some cases He may have something better in store for you, and sometimes it is that dreaded word 'Wait'.

2 Peter 3:8 NIV: "But do not forget this one thing, dear friends: With the Lord a day is like a thousand years, and a thousand years are like a day.

So, to us, every minute seems like such a long, long, time, but on God's timetable, no time at all. I hope that makes sense to you, but, if not, I have great news for you.

Luke 21:25–28 NIV: "There will be signs in the sun, moon and stars. On the earth, nations will be in anguish and perplexity at the roaring and tossing of the sea. People will faint from terror, apprehensive of what is coming on the world, for the heavenly bodies will be shaken. At that time, they will see the Son of Man coming in a cloud with power and great glory. When these things begin to take place, stand up and lift up your heads, because your redemption is drawing near."

Of course, that is only for the saved, but what about the non-believers?

1 Timothy 2:3–8 NIV: "This is good, and pleases God our Savior, Who wants all people to be saved and to come to a knowledge of the truth. For there is one God and one Mediator between God and mankind, the man Christ Jesus, Who gave Himself as a ransom for all people. This has now been witnessed to at the proper time. And for this purpose, I was appointed a herald and an apostle—I am telling the truth, I am not lying—and a true and faithful teacher of the Gentiles.

Therefore, I want the men everywhere to pray, lifting up holy hands without anger or disputing."

It is so crystal clear what this book is trying to tell us. Even the blind, after hearing the word, and little children, at an early age, have acknowledged the truth, and love of Jesus Christ. What are you waiting for, I promise, we are not guaranteed the next day of living on this earth.

James 4:13-14 KJV: Go to now, ye that say, To day or to morrow we will go into such a city, and continue there a year, and buy and sell, and get gain: Whereas ye know not what shall be on the morrow. For what is your life? It is even a vapour, that appeareth for a little time, and then vanisheth away."

The Bible is telling us, you may not be here tomorrow. For you non-believers, which is it? Heaven or Hell? You have the free will to make that choice. My hope is that, after reading this book, it will not be the wrong one! If you want a place in Heaven, please jump to the last chapter, you can always come back to where you are reading. Do not wait. There are no promises of a long life here on earth. Do Not Hesitate!

Footprints In The Sand

Written by Mary Stevenson (1936)

One night I dreamed I was walking along the beach with the Lord.
Many scenes from my life flashed across the sky.
In each scene I noticed footprints in the sand.
Sometimes there were two sets of footprints, other times there was one only.
This bothered me because I noticed that during the low periods of my life,
when I was suffering from anguish, sorrow or defeat, I could see only one
set of footprints, so I said to the Lord;
"You promised me Lord, that if I followed you, you would walk with me
always. But I have noticed that during the most trying periods of my life
there has only been one set of footprints in the sand. Why, when I needed
you most, have you not been there for me?"
The Lord replied, "The years when you have seen only one set of foot-
prints, my child, is when I carried you."

Joy, Thanksgiving, and the Agape Kind Of Love

I deliberately put these three topics together, because they are positive things we really need to know in our Christian walk. Let's start with the latter word first.

The word "Love" is used too loosely in our daily language. I love that dress, certain kinds of foods, flowers, scenery, animals, people (Sometimes confused with the word 'Lust'). Needless to say, it is commonly used in almost everything in some form or another. But let us refine it to the purest, finest kind of love, and that is the 'Agape' kind of love, or the Godly kind of love.

Wikipedia's definition of the word Agape: "love: the highest form of love, charity; the love of God for man and of man for God."

This is the type of love to be used when I talk about "Joy", and "Thanksgiving". Let's start with the meaning of the word "Joy", and what God has to say about it. True joy comes from our Lord. There are so many Scriptures in the Bible on this topic, I thought I would just mention two.

Webster's dictionary describes "Joy" as: "the emotion evoked by well-being, success, or good fortune or by the prospect of possessing what one desires."

Romans 12:12 NIV: "Be joyful in hope, patient in affliction, faithful in prayer."

Neh. 8:10 NIV: "Nehemiah said, "Go and enjoy choice food and sweet drinks, and send some to those who have nothing prepared. This day is holy to our Lord. Do not grieve, for the joy of the LORD is your strength."

This should be the order in which you should use the Agape kind of love. Of course, Jesus should be, and always will be, number one in your life.

1. J is for 'Jesus'
2. O is for your family and friends.
3. Y is for yourself

The third one, yourself, (myself) was by far the hardest for me to forgive. The others were quite simple. Before becoming a Christian, I lived a very sinful, wretched life that I have talked about before.

Once again, if you need to, the "Sinner's Prayer" is in the last chapter. Webster's dictionary defines "Thanksgiving" as:

1. a public acknowledgment or celebration of divine goodness
2. the act of giving thanks
3. a prayer expressing gratitude

Now some of the Scriptures on "Thanksgiving".

Chronicles 16:8 KJV: "Oh give thanks to the LORD; call upon His name; make known His deeds among the peoples!"

Chronicles 16:34 KJV: "Oh give thanks to the LORD, for He is good; for His steadfast love endures forever!"

Psalm 9:1 KJV: "I will give thanks to the LORD with my whole heart; I will recount all of your wonderful deeds."

Psalm 69:30 KJV: "I will praise the name of God with a song; I will magnify Him with thanksgiving."

These are just a few of the many beautifully written scriptures on the subject. In November, December, and January, when I go to nursing homes, I talk about the three types of giving.

1. November: Giving thanks to God.
2. December: Giving to others. Especially those priceless gifts (see below).

Priceless Gifts

People are always giving material gifts for Birthdays, Holidays, Graduations, Anniversaries, etc. This is all well and good, but what about all those "Priceless Gifts"? Everywhere I go, I talk about all those precious, priceless gifts. What are these gifts that you cannot put a price on? These are the gifts from the heart. A kind word, a smile, a hug, talk to someone, listen to them, pray for them, tell them they look nice, witness to them, and most of all, tell them that you love them. For years, I have been doing this, and encouraging others to do the same. Try it! You will be surprised at the difference it makes, especially to those you may not even know who are hurting inside.

3. And lastly, January: The art of "Forgiving". God dictates that we must forgive others, as hard as it may be in some cases, before He will forgive us.

Matthew 6:14-15 NIV: "For if you forgive other people when they sin against you, your heavenly Father will also forgive you. But if you do not forgive others their sins, your Father will not forgive your sins."

And finally, Matthew 18:21-22 NIV: "Then Peter came to Jesus and asked, 'Lord, how many times shall I forgive my brother or sister who sins against me? Up to seven times?' Jesus answered, 'I tell you, not seven times, but seventy-seven times.'"

Like many topics we will be talking about, there are so many relevant Scriptures, along with all my comments, that it would take a massive number of books to put it all in.

Are We Truly Thankful/Grateful? (All below is :)

1. 1 Thessalonians 5:18 ESV: "Give thanks in all circumstances; for this is the will of God in Christ Jesus for you."
2. Psalm 107:1 ESV: "Oh give thanks to the Lord, for He is good, for His steadfast love endures forever!"
3. Ephesians 5:20 ESV: "Giving thanks always and for everything to God the Father in the name of our Lord Jesus Christ."
4. Colossians 3:15-17 ESV: "And let the peace of Christ rule in your hearts, to which indeed you were called in one body. And be thankful. Let the word of Christ dwell in you richly, teaching and admonishing one another in all wisdom, singing psalms and hymns and spiritual songs, with thankfulness in your hearts to God. And whatever you do, in word or deed, do everything in the name of the Lord Jesus, giving thanks to God the Father through Him."
5. James 1:17 ESV: "Every good gift and every perfect gift is from above, coming down from the Father of lights with whom there is no variation or shadow due to change."
6. Philippians 4:6 ESV: "Do not be anxious about anything, but in everything by prayer and supplication with thanksgiving let your requests be made known to God."
7. 2 Corinthians 9:15 ESV: "Thanks be to God for His inexpressible gift!"
8. Psalm 106:1 ESV: "Praise the Lord! Oh give thanks to the Lord, for He is good, for His steadfast love endures forever!"
9. Psalm 105:1 ESV: "Oh give thanks to the Lord; call upon His name; make known His deeds among the peoples!"
10. Colossians 3:15 ESV: "And let the peace of Christ rule in your hearts, to which indeed you were called in one body. And be thankful."
11. Colossians 4:2 ESV: "Continue steadfastly in prayer, being

watchful in it with thanksgiving."

12. Psalm 118:1-18 "Oh give thanks to the Lord, for He is good; for His steadfast love endures forever! Let Israel say, 'His steadfast love endures forever.' Let the house of Aaron say, 'His steadfast love endures forever.' Let those who fear the Lord say, 'His steadfast love endures forever.' Out of my distress I called on the Lord; the Lord answered me and set me free."

13. Psalm 20:4 ESV: "May He grant you your heart's desire and fulfill all your plans!"

14. Psalm 30:12 ESV: "That my glory may sing your praise and not be silent. O Lord my God, I will give thanks to You forever!"

15. Colossians 3:17 ESV: "And whatever you do, in word or deed, do everything in the name of the Lord Jesus, giving thanks to God the Father through Him."

16. Romans 1:21 ESV: "For although they knew God, they did not honor Him as God or give thanks to Him, but they became futile in their thinking, and their foolish hearts were darkened."

17. Psalm 100:4 ESV: "Enter His gates with thanksgiving, and His courts with praise! Give thanks to Him; bless His name!"

18. Isaiah 12:4-5 ESV: "And you will say in that day: "Give thanks to the Lord, call upon His name, make known His deeds among the peoples, proclaim that His name is exalted. "Sing praises to the Lord, for He has done gloriously; let this be made known in all the earth."

19. 1 Chronicles 29:13 ESV: "And now we thank you, our God, and praise your glorious name."

20. Philemon 1:4 ESV: "I thank my God always when I remember You're in my prayers."

Christians Anonymous
to the Believers

For quite some time now, we have had groups such as A.A. (Alcoholics Anonymous), N.A. (Narcotics Anonymous), Both of which I belonged to in the earlier years of my life. There is also O.E. (Overeaters Anonymous), one for sex addicts, and probably many more I never even heard of.

Now what I think is, that we should start one called C.A. (Christians Anonymous). I feel that many Christians need to join this new group. I firmly believe that less than one percent of Christians out there are witnessing and inviting people to church. If this is ruffling some of your feathers, then I am sorry, but I truly believe we all need to check out our walk with God. I imagine C.A. would probably have more members than all the others combined. I can see myself on stage, at my first meeting, with the microphone on high, and me softly speaking (Where no one can hear me.) saying with my head bowed: "My name is Lloyd, and I am a Christian." Then the crowd softly saying, with their heads down: "Hi Lloyd". So many Christians act like they are ashamed of what we know is true. Let's see what the Bible says on this. It is what we call "The Great Commission".

Matthew 28:18-20 NIV: "Then Jesus came to them and said, 'All authority in heaven and on earth has been given to Me. Therefore, go and make disciples of all nations, baptizing them in the name of the Father and of the Son and of the Holy Spirit, and teaching them to obey everything I have commanded you. And surely I am with you always, to the very end of the age.'"

Years ago, I paid for an ad, that viewed on many of the stations on free television from 6.1 all the way to 6.7. I paid for only one year, but they ran it at least two or three years without asking for more money after that year was up…unless they are still running it now. It went something like this:

You see three crosses on a hill, on a cloudy day, that fade out, and came back in. Someone is singing the Old Rugged Cross in the background. The ad said—and I was talking to the believers only:

"Jesus died for you on the cross. What have you done for Him lately. Touch someone with the love, and the Gospel, of Jesus Christ." Then it mentioned my ministry. Reach Out Ministry. I did not put an address, phone number, or email address nor did I ask for any money. I just wanted to inspire Christians to do more for the Lord, and every day, or week, when possible. Did it work at all? Who knows.

Do you know, in a sense that we are all ministers. Not as pastors, but in our everyday life.

2 Corinthians 3:6 NLT: "He has enabled us to be ministers of His new covenant. This is a covenant not of written laws, but of the Spirit. The old written covenant ends in death; but under the new covenant, the Spirit gives life. His name is Jesus."

Is this talking to a certain few? No, it is speaking to all Christians. I have certain things that I do that God has put in my heart. I have a black leather vest that I wear most of the time, in all kinds of weather. On the back, in big print, at the top and bottom it says: "Jesus Forever", and in the middle of this is a big cross. On the top on one side is the fish. The fish symbol represents the acrostic and symbolizes salvation in Christ through water baptism—fish are saved in water, and we are saved in water through Jesus. On the other side is my name, with the name "Reach Out Ministries," and an eagle in the middle. I use that a lot because of scripture:

Isaiah 40:31 NIV: "but those who hope in the LORD will renew their strength. They will soar on wings like eagles; they will run and not grow weary, they will walk and not be faint."

Then on the bottom two sides, one says: "Got Jesus", and the other, "Christians aren't perfect, just forgiven". The funniest thing about this, about 70% of the people who come up to me ask: "Are You a biker?". I call this jacket my "Silent Witness". There are many other ways to witness. I have bought thousands of Bibles through the ministry God has so graciously given me, and I give them to anyone, any group, organization, or church that will take them. I buy them by the cases and the cheapest place I have found so far is a company on the internet that goes by the initials B.B.T.C. I am not plugging these people so I will not give you their complete name. Maybe you can find someone cheaper. To date I have not. I also buy thousands of crosses, (Without Jesus on it, as He has been resurrected.) from a company with the initials O.T. When I go anywhere, out to eat, cruises, etc., I hand many out. I tell the person, waitress, whoever, that I want to give them the best gift they will ever receive. As they smile and reach out to grab it, I tell them not this, but the One who it represents. I know you know, but I will say it anyway. For Who? His name is Jesus! Use one of my ideas or find one of your own ways to show your love. Let's make a difference.

The Wings of an Eagle

Scripture of Faith, and Encouragement

Isaiah 40:29–31 KJV

He giveth power to the faint;
and to them that have no might He increaseth strength.
Even the youths shall faint and be weary, and the young men shall utterly fall:
But they that wait upon the LORD shall renew [their] strength;
they shall mount up with wings as eagles;
they shall run, and not be weary;
[and] they shall walk, and not faint.

Ark Of The Covenant

Believe This Or Not

Many years ago, when I was going to school to be a minister, I was a regular at a certain church where, on one Sunday, had a special black Evangelist talk to the congregation. What he said should really astound you, and I believe this is only something God would do. If I remember right, he was in Israel helping with an excavation, and somehow during that time got connected with the inner circle, who knew where the Ark was and information about it. As goose bumps went up and down my arm, he explained three things.

1. The Ark Of The Covenant has been found.
2. It was in a cave, under where Jesus was crucified.
3. They tested His blood and it only had the "X' chromosome, on the mercy seat, whereas we have either the "XX", or "XY".

Wikipedia says this about chromosomes:
Females typically have two of the same kind of sex chromosome (XX) and are called the homogametic sex. Males typically have two different kinds of sex chromosomes (XY) and are called the heterogametic sex.

This being the blood of Jesus, He could not have the XY chromosome, or He would not have been born of a virgin. Now how would this be possible?

John 19:33-34 NIV: "But when they came to Jesus and found that He was already dead, they did not break His legs. Instead, one of the soldiers pierced Jesus' side with a spear, bringing a sudden flow of blood and water."

Matthew 27:51 KJV: "And, behold, the veil of the temple was rent in twain from the top to the bottom; and the earth did quake, and the rocks rent."

In other words, they are talking about an earthquake, and the rocks split (rent) in half. This had to happen, in order for His blood to fall on the mercy seat in place of the animal's blood as in the past, which only *covered* the sins. Although there is much said about all this in the Bible, especially Jesus forgiving our sins to never be remembered.

Talking about animal's blood only covers the sin:

Hebrews 10:4 NIV: "it is impossible for the blood of bulls and goats to take away sins."

Talking about Jesus and that He can, and will forgive sins:

1 John 1:9 NIV: "If we confess our sins, He is faithful and just to forgive us [our] sins, and to cleanse us from all unrighteousness."

1 John 1:17 KJV: But if we walk in the light, as He is in the light, we have fellowship one with another, and the blood of Jesus Christ His Son cleanseth us from all sin."

So, if the "ARK" was in a cave, under where Jesus died, how would it have gotten the blood on the Mercy Seat? Of course, God had it placed in the exact spot for this to happen.

So, putting everything together, the blood that flowed from His body, and through the cracks of the rocks, and earth to the mercy seat, to complete His sacrifice for us. My God is a God of perfection and completion, and this would have had to happen, to replace the blood of the animals of the past.

Do you believe this could have happened? I truly believe this is what happened, and why the scripture reads as it does, to fulfill Jesus role as our "Sacrificial Lamb".

I, personally, do not deserve you to die for me, Jesus, but I am eternally grateful. I love you, my Lord, and Savior Jesus, Christ!

Acts Of Random Kindness (ARK)

So much is going on in this world, with people going hungry, no shoes, and no place to stay…well I think you know where I am going with this. Did Jesus have an opinion on helping others? Let's see.

Matthew 10:4 NIV: "And if anyone gives even a cup of cold water to one of these little ones who is My disciple, truly I tell you, that person will certainly not lose their reward."

This scripture means not just water. It can be money, food, manual labor, and anything we can do to help others. But there are pitfalls to helping others, as many will take advantage of people's generosity, and by doing so, they are hindering the many out there who really need the help. A pastor taught me something he called "Red Flags". I was in his office one day, and a lady was asking for help. Sounds alright so far, right? Wrong. The pastor after talking to her for a little bit, found out she lived about 20 miles from his church. With so many churches so much closer to her, she was probably making the rounds of ones farther away. Why? Probably because she went to the ones closer to her for help and they finally decided that they had given her all the help they could and would focus on helping others probably less fortunate. I think you catch my drift. So, am I telling you not to help someone?

No, sometimes you have to be more selective and do a little homework to find those more deserving. I will tell you of two other cases, and just drop it there. A gentlemen came into a church before the service wanting to buy gas for him, and his family of three, to go see his dying brother. The church said they would see what they could do after service. He, and his family, did not attend service, but came in after it was over. The deacons, and church, decided to help anyway, but one of the deacons would have to go to the station with him, and pay with the church credit card. The guy suddenly admitted he had a full tank. Hard telling what he really wanted that money for. The last one was when my car broke down in downtown Nashville, and a passerby helped me push my car to the side of the road. He told me he had not eaten for three days, and I could tell, by his energy in helping and the look on his face, that he was lying. Being kind enough to help me, I gave him three certificates for a free hamburger each, that McDonalds has so graciously donated to my ministry for almost the entire 28 years it has been in existence. Thank you, McDonalds! He took them, but then his story changed and he said he needed some ointment for some kind of rash that he had. I did not ask to see the rash, but when I told him I already filled the need he had originally asked me for he became very loud and persistent about it and would not leave. This continued until a policeman came over to see if everything was alright. The man in need left in a hurry. Thanks to all the men and women in blue who put their lives on the line every day. Also, thanks to the military, the fire departments, Christian missionaries, and so many more. Although I have many more stories I could tell you, that is where I will stop. So, am I telling you not to help others? Not at all. I will though, give you some of the best pointers I can. If someone has a need, and the person seems to be legit, fulfill it if you can. God does not expect you to help everyone out there, no one has all that kind of money. If you find out later you got burnt, as I have so many times in the past, forgive that person, and God will still honor what you did, and dishonor the one who lied to you. In fact, a lot of needs out there will not cost you a cent, like cutting an elderly person's grass, and other blessings you can bestow upon people that just need physical help. There is an expression, "Pay It Forward," that is, if someone blesses you in your time of need, you should do something nice for someone else. It's tough, these days, to know if someone truly needs help or not, but do not close the door. You never know when it may be your turn to need someone else's help. Go out and start making a positive difference in the troubled world we live in. Your help will be appreciated and rewarded. May God Bless You for all you do!

Words of Wisdom for Christians and Non-Christians

1. People do not care what you know, until they know that you care.
2. In life, if you go three steps forward, and not more than two steps back, you will always get ahead.
3. It is not rather you talk the talk, but rather you walk the walk.
4. People say how awesome and great our God is, but personally, I do not believe we have a word in our English language to tell how awesome and great He truly is.
5. In proving the Bible is real, pull up on the internet, Chariot Wheels in the Red Sea, and you can also see a video on it. Scripture about how God saved the Israelites from the Egyptians, who were out to destroy Moses, and the Jewish people, who left with him out of Egypt.
6. Exodus 15:3-5 KJV: "The LORD is a man of war: the LORD is His name. Pharaoh's chariots and his host hath He cast into the sea: his chosen captains also are drowned in the Red sea. The depths have covered them: they sank into the bottom as a stone."

7. Did you know? I was watching a documentary a few years back and they said that: Old Faithful, the geyser everyone loves to visit in Yellowstone National Park, will be the biggest eruption the world has ever seen. He said he did not know when, but definitely will happen.
8. Why did Jesus have to be born in Bethlehem? Bethlehem means "House Of Bread", and Jesus is the 'Bread Of Life".
9. Do your research and check on the internet. as many believe they have found Noah's Ark on Mount Ararat, in Turkey.
10. On the lighter side. They have a complete replica of Noah's Ark in Kentucky. After going there, I found out that Noah did not have it that bad. It had air-conditioning, television, gift shop, and a snack bar. L.O.L.
11. I heard someone say, the worst thing in life you can do is try to please everybody. That is true, except in the case of God.
12. One time I saw this sign: "Lord, make today my words sweet as honey, for tomorrow I may eat them."
13. People are saying that all roads lead to God, and they are right.

Romans 14:11 NIV: "It is written: 'As surely as I live,' says the Lord, 'every knee will bow before me; every tongue will acknowledge God.'"

Matthew 7:13-14 NIV: "Enter through the narrow gate. For wide is the gate and broad is the road that leads to destruction, and many enter through it. But small is the gate and narrow the road that leads to life, and only a few find it."

Let me close with this:

The Serenity Prayer
God grant me the serenity to accept the things I cannot change,
the courage to change the things I can,
and the wisdom to know the difference.

Did Ya Know?

Bugs

Did you know, that these gruesome awful creatures that we slap at, kill with bug lights, and use all kinds of chemicals to keep off of us, may not be as bad as we all think. Believe it or not, when God told the children of Israel, in the Old Testament, of what they can, and cannot eat, He mentioned some bugs. Does that sound tempting and tasty? As for me, I have not tried any, except those that inadvertently got in my mouth while talking too much, which I do a lot. If God says it is okay, then it is okay with me. Besides, I hear they have a lot of protein, which is good for you.

Leviticus 11:20–23 NIV: "All flying insects that walk on six legs are to be regarded as unclean by you. There are, however, some flying insects that walk on six legs that you may eat: those that have jointed legs for hopping on the ground. Of these you may eat any kind of locust, katydid, cricket, or grasshopper. But all other flying insects that have six legs you are to regard as unclean."

Now are you thinking about going out a catching a few for your dinner meal? Not?

Mark 1:6 NIV: "John wore clothing made of camel's hair, with a leather belt around his waist, and he ate locusts and wild honey."

Well if John The Baptist can add some honey to flavor it, I guess it may go down a bit smoother. Not to gross anyone out, but I am not sure I would enjoy talking to someone who had one of these scrumptious meals, and still had legs, or body parts stuck between their teeth. L.O.L.

Simon Called Peter

Did you realize that Peter was destined for hell had it not been for Jesus? First, he denied Jesus three times.

John 18:16–17 NIV: "but Peter had to wait outside at the door. The other disciple, who was known to the high priest, came back, spoke to the servant girl on duty, and brought Peter in. 'You aren't one of this Man's disciples too, are you?' she asked Peter. He replied, 'I am not.'

That was the first denial. Here is the second.

John 18:25 NIV: "Meanwhile, Simon Peter was still standing there warming himself. So they asked him, 'You aren't one of His disciples too, are you?' He denied it, saying, 'I am not.'

Now, remember I said three times?

John 18:26–27 NIV: "One of the high priest's servants, a relative of the man whose ear Peter had cut off, challenged him, 'Didn't I see you with Him in the garden?' Again, Peter denied it, and at that moment a rooster began to crow."

Now this where it gets interesting. Jesus counteracted those three denials with the scriptures of feeding my sheep three times to Peter. I will tell you why.

John 21:15-17 NIV: "When they had finished eating, Jesus said to Simon Peter, 'Simon son of John, do you love Me more than these?'

'Yes, Lord,' he said, 'You know that I love you.' Jesus said, 'Feed My lambs.' Again, Jesus said, 'Simon son of John, do you love Me?' He answered, 'Yes, Lord, you know that I love You.' Jesus said, 'Take care of My sheep.' The third time He said to him, 'Simon son of John, do you love Me?' Peter was hurt because Jesus asked him the third time, 'Do you love Me?' He said, 'Lord, you know all things; You know that I love You.' Jesus said, 'Feed My sheep.'"

In one version it is said that Simon Peter was deeply hurt, and another that he grieved. Sometimes, I wonder if Simon Peter thought back to the time he denied Jesus three times, and actually knew why Jesus had to do this three times to cancel out the three denials he had made. Maybe he even thought of what Jesus said before the denials. Now, I told you I would tell you why this came about, so here it is.

Luke 22:31-32 NIV: "Simon, Simon, Satan has asked to sift all of you as wheat. But I have prayed for you, Simon, that your faith may not fail. And when you have turned back, strengthen your brothers."

You see, Satan wanted Simon Peter even before the denials, but after he did deny Jesus three times, Satan had good reason to petition his case to God to get Simon Peter's soul. Jesus, of course, had other ideas, and knew that Simon Peter would be a strong advocate for the Kingdom Of God. So, I am sure Jesus prayed for him again, plus He asked Simon Peter three times to find out where his heart was and He knew at that time that his heart was true. If you wonder if Jesus made a good decision on that, study up on Simon Peter, and find out how a great man of God he finally became.

Just One More Soul

The preachers are weary
The singers are tired
The church as we know it
Is losing its fire
Some are discouraged from bearing the load
But we must determine to keep pressing on
'Cause if just one more soul
Were to walk down the aisle
It would be worth every struggle
It would be worth every mile
A lifetime of labor is still worth it all
If it rescues just one more soul
So preachers, keep preachin'
And singers, go sing
Laymen, keep sharing
That Jesus is King
The angels have gathered, they're surrounding the throne
And they'll start rejoicing for just one more soul.

Author unknown

He Is Risen

Jesus had not servants, yet they called Him Master
Had no degree, yet they called Him Teacher
Had no medicines, Yet they called Him Healer
He had no army, yet kings feared Him
He won no military battle, yet He conquered the world
He committed no crime, yet they crucified Him
He was buried in a tomb, het He lives today!

Author Unknown

True Sadness of This World

When I first read this, it totally broke my heart, and even now, after all these years, it is still powerful. For anyone who is not moved, you must have a cold, cold heart. This is not something someone just wrote to be writing, it is full of major tragedies throughout this world. It makes me want to cry knowing everything written is actual fact.

To the American People

While you were sleeping soundly in your bed,
another Christian was buried alive.
While you were having your morning coffee,
another Christian was beheaded.
While you were having a tasty lunch,
another Christian boy's eyes were gouged out.
While you were eating a wonderful dinner,
another Christian was crucified.
While you were having an evening snack,
another Christian girl was kidnapped and raped.
And the Christians cry out for the Americans to come and help them

and there is a deafening silence.

And no help comes from America and the Lord Jesus up in Heaven above was quite angry because no help came from America to aid their Christian brothers and sisters.

And the hate goes on and on. And the killing goes on and on.

When will it ever end?

Come soon, Lord Jesus!

Author unknown

Politically Correct Santa

'Twas the night before Christmas and Santa's a wreck...
How to live in a world that's politically correct?
His workers no longer would answer to "Elves",
"Vertically Challenged" they were calling themselves.
And labor conditions at the North Pole
Were alleged by the union to stifle the soul.
Four reindeer had vanished, without much propriety,
Released to the wilds by the Humane Society.
And equal employment had made it quite clear
That Santa had better not use just reindeer.
So Dancer and Donner, Comet and Cupid,
Were replaced with 4 pigs, and you know that looked stupid!?
The runners had been removed from his sleigh;
The ruts were termed dangerous by the E.P.A.
And people had started to call for the cops
When they heard sled noises on their roof-tops.
Second-hand smoke from his pipe had his workers quite frightened.
His fur trimmed red suit was called "Unenlightened."
And to show you the strangeness of life's ebbs and flows:
Rudolf was suing over unauthorized use of his nose
And had gone on Geraldo, in front of the nation,

Demanding millions in over-due compensation.
So, half of the reindeer were gone; and his wife, .
Who suddenly said she'd enough of this life,
Joined a self-help group, packed, and left in a whiz,
Demanding from now on her title was Ms.
And as for the gifts, why, he'd ne'er had a notion
That making a choice could cause so much commotion.
Nothing of leather, nothing of fur,
Which meant nothing for him. And nothing for her.
Nothing that might be construed to pollute.
Nothing to aim. Nothing to shoot.
Nothing that clamored or made lots of noise.
Nothing for just girls. Or just for the boys.
Nothing that claimed to be gender specific.
Nothing that's warlike or non-pacific.
No candy or sweets…they were bad for the tooth.
Nothing that seemed to embellish a truth.
And fairy tales, while not yet forbidden,
Were like Ken and Barbie, better off hidden.
For they raised the hackles of those psychological
Who claimed the only good gift was one ecological.
No baseball, no football…someone could get hurt;
Besides, playing sports exposed kids to dirt.
Dolls were said to be sexist, and should be passé;
And Nintendo would rot your entire brain away.
So Santa just stood there, disheveled, perplexed;
He just could not figure out what to do next.
He tried to be merry, tried to be gay,
But you've got to be careful with that word today.
His sack was quite empty, limp to the ground;
Nothing fully acceptable was to be found.
Something special was needed, a gift that he might

Give to all without angering the left or the right.
A gift that would satisfy, with no indecision,
Each group of people, every religion;
Every ethnicity, every hue,
Everyone, everywhere…even you.
So here is that gift, it's price beyond worth…
May you and your loved ones enjoy peace on earth.

Author Unknown

This is humorous, but so much truth in what the author is saying.

Christian Children Say the Funniest Things

These are all true stories

1. After the christening of his baby brother in church, Jason sobbed all the way home in the back seat of the car. His father asked him three times what was wrong. Finally, the boy replied, "That preacher said he wanted us brought up in a Christian home, and I wanted to stay with you guys."

2. Six-year-old Angie and her four-year-old brother Joel were sitting together in church. Joel giggled, sang, and talked out loud. Finally, his big sister had had enough. "You're not supposed to talk out loud in church." "Why? Who's going to stop me?" Joel asked. Angie pointed to the back of the church and said, "See those two men standing by the door? They're hushers."

3. A Sunday school teacher asked her children, as they were on the way to church service, "And why is it necessary to be quiet in church?" One bright little girl replied, "Because people are sleeping."

4. A Sunday school teacher was discussing the Ten Commandments

with her five- and six-year olds. After explaining the command-ment to "Honor thy Father and thy Mother", she asked, "Is there a commandment that teaches us how to treat our broth-ers and sisters?" Without missing a beat one little boy (the old-est of a family) answered, "Thou shall not kill."

5. One day a little girl was sitting and watching her mother do the dishes at the kitchen sink. She suddenly noticed that her moth-er had several strands of white hair sticking out from her oth-erwise brown hair. She looked at her mother and inquisitively asked, "Why are some of your hairs white, Mom?" Her mother replied, "Well, every time that you do something wrong and make me cry or unhappy, one of my hairs turns white." The little girl thought about this revelation for a moment, then said, "Momma, how come ALL of grandma's hairs are white?"

6. The children were lined up in the cafeteria of a Catholic el-ementary school for lunch. At the head of the table was a large pile of apples. The nun posted a note on the apple tray: "Take only ONE. God is watching." Moving further along the lunch line, at the other end of the table was a large pile of chocolate chip cookies. A child had written a note, "Take all you want. God is watching the apples."

7. A little girl was talking to her teacher about whales. The teacher said it was physically impossible for a whale to swallow a hu-man because even though it was a very large mammal its throat was very small. The little girl stated that Jonah was swallowed by a whale. Irritated, the teacher reiterated that a whale could not swallow a human; it was physically impossible. The little girl said, "When I get to heaven I will ask Jonah." The teacher asked, "What if Jonah went to hell?" The little girl replied, "Then you ask him."

8. A little boy walked down the beach, and as he did, he spied a matronly woman sitting under a beach umbrella on the sand.

He walked up to her and asked, "Are you a Christian?" "Yes, she said." "Do you read your Bible every day?" She nodded her head, "Yes." "Do you pray often?" the boy asked next, and again she answered, "Yes." With that he asked his final question. "Will you hold my quarter while I go swimming?"

9. A father was reading Bible stories to his young son. He read, "The man named Lot was warned to take his wife and flee out of the city, but his wife looked back and was turned to salt." His son asked, "What happened to the flea?"

10. Casey asked her Sunday School teacher a question: "If the people of Israel are Israelites, and the people of Canaan are Canaanites, are the people of Paris called Parasites?"

True Mistakes Made
In Church Bulletins

1. Life groups meet on Wednesday evening at 7:00 PM for food, fun, and fellowwhipping.
2. Announcement in the church bulletin for a National PRAYER & FASTING Conference: "The cost for attending the Fasting and Prayer conference includes meals."
3. "Ladies, don't forget the rummage sale. It's a chance to get rid of those things not worth keeping around the house. Don't forget your husbands."
4. The peacemaking meeting scheduled for today has been cancelled due to a conflict.
5. The sermon this morning: "Jesus Walks on the Water." The sermon tonight: "Searching for Jesus."
6. Don't let worry kill you off—let the Church help.
7. The senior choir invites any member of the congregation who enjoys sinning to join the choir.
8. For those of you who have children and don't know it, we have a nursery downstairs.
9. This evening at 7 PM there will be a hymn singing in the park across from the Church. Bring a blanket and come prepared to sin.

10. The pastor would appreciate it if the ladies of the congregation would lend him their electric girdles for the pancake breakfast next Sunday.
11. Low Self Esteem Support Group will meet Thursday at 7 PM. Please use the back door.
12. Weight Watchers will meet at 7 PM at the First Presbyterian Church. Please use large double door at the side entrance.
13. Thursday night-Potluck Supper. Prayer and medication to follow.
14. The rosebud on the alter this morning is to announce the birth of David Alan Belzer, the sin of Rev. and Mrs. Belzer.
15. This afternoon there will be a meeting in the south and north ends of the church. Children will be baptized at both ends.
16. Evening massage—6 pm.
17. The third verse of "Blessed Assurance" will be sung without musical accomplishment.
18. Remember in prayer the many who are sick of our church and the community.
19. Next Sunday, a special collection will be taken to defray the cost of the new carpet. All those wishing to do something on the new carpet will come forward and get a piece of paper.
20. Barbara remains in the hospital and needs blood donors for more transfusions. She is also having trouble sleeping and requests tapes of Pastor Jack's sermons.
21. The outreach committee has enlisted 25 visitors to make calls on people who are not afflicted with any church.

Church Signs and Sayings

1. Come as you are…you can change inside.
2. Get off the fence and under The Cross. It's much safer.
3. Better is 1 Day at The Lord's House than 10,000 Days at the Lake.
4. Tomorrow's forecast: God reigns and the Son shines!
5. Why pay for GPS? Jesus gives directions for free.
6. Need a lifeguard? Ours walks on water!
7. Honk if you love Jesus…Text while driving if you want to meet Him.
8. God will accept broken hearts—but you must give Him all the pieces!
9. If the devil is knocking at your front door, let Jesus answer it!
10. God expects spiritual fruit, not religious nuts!
11. When you throw mud at someone, you're the one losing ground!
12. May all your days have Son shine!
13. The 10 Commandments are not multiple choice!
14. The 10 Commandments are not 10 suggestions!
15. Church sign—ATM inside: Atonement, Truth, Mercy.
16. "I'm also making a list and checking it twice"—God.
17. God does not believe in atheists—therefore atheists do not exist.
18. Do not criticize your wife's judgment. See who she married.
19. Forbidden fruits create many jams.

20. For God so loved the world, that He didn't send a committee.
21. Don't give up! Moses was once a basket-case too!
22. There will be a separation of church and state—the rapture!
23. Noah should have swatted the 2 mosquitoes!
24. The best vitamin for a Christian is B1.
25. Friends don't let Friends die without Jesus.
26. True independence is dependence on Jesus.
27. Choose the "Bread of Life", or you are toast.
28. If you don't like the way you were born, try being born again!
29. Need a new life? God accepts trade-ins!
30. Lost? Try GPS—God's Plan of Salvation!
31. Jesus is an investment that never loses!
32. Try Jesus! If you don't like Him, the devil will gladly take you back!
33. Faithbook: Jesus has sent you a friend request.
34. Jesus loves You...and He approves this message!
35. God's answers are wiser than our prayers!
36. 7 days without Prayer makes one WEAK!
37. Church sign—Our Church is Prayer Conditioned!
38. A family alter can alter a family!
39. P.U.S.H. = Pray Until Something Happens!
40. Prayer—the ultimate wireless connection!
41. Prayer—Free wireless connection to God with no roaming fees!
42. God answers all knee mail.
43. Can't sleep? Don't count sheep—talk to the shepherd!
44. Church is like fudge...sweet, with a few nuts!
45. For Home Improvement—Bring the Family to Church.
46. The church is a gift from God. Some assembly required.
47. Shock your Mom...go to church today!
48. Church sign—we are not Dairy Queen...but, we have Great Sundays!
49. Need a lifeguard? Ours walks on water!
50. What on earth are you doing for Heaven's sake!

Murder In The First Degree: Abortion!

The verdict is out and has been out for thousands of years from an eternal God. God is tough on this matter, and rightly so. Abortion is "Murder In The First Degree!" First of all, let me say, this is one of the hardest topics for me to write. As harsh as it may sound, I will never take it back. In the Old Testament, and I hear, even now, people sacrificed children to a false god, or a want-to-be god, called 'Satin'. This is what we are doing, murdering innocent, helpless babies who cannot speak for themselves. If you have had an abortion, or you had played a part in an abortion, my God can and will forgive you. If you are a doctor, nurse, councilor for abortion, do literature, or even a janitor at these places. Quit, and quit now! As for those who are thinking about having an abortion, by all that is Holy, and the words of our Living God, PLEASE DO NOT!!! I have seen talk shows, and documentaries that show women who feel a void in their life, regret, uncontrolled crying spells, emptiness, and maybe some even suicidal because of it. There was a documentary done in 1984 called *The Silent Scream*. The film depicts the abortion process via ultrasound, and shows an abortion taking place in the uterus. During the abortion process, the fetus is described as appearing to make outcries of pain and discomfort. You need to watch this, if you have the stomach for it, as I do not, and have seen just a little of it. It just made me sick and left an impact. There is still a vivid picture in my mind. The face of this baby looked just like the face in the horror movie *Scream*. Not to go into a lot of what this movie is about, but it shows the silent scream of a baby as they pull the legs, and arms, off of them. This should almost make you sick just to think about it. I also understand that they use these babies for experiments and sell baby parts. How evil has this world truly become? Before telling you what God says, let me give you a little more insight, as these precious children of God are being slaughtered as if they were chickens for an evening meal. Each one of these babies has a heart, soul, mind, and body. Why should we be allowed to destroy these delicate, fragile, lives. They are not just a glob of flesh to destroy at will. That is doing the devil's work.

John 10:10 NIV: (Jesus talking about the devil.) "The thief comes only to steal and kill and destroy; I have come that they may have life and have it to the full."

Below is from Wise Geek on the internet who proves these babies are living, loving human beings, just wanting to born and loved back. What kind of love are we showing the world, and our children, when we commit such heinous crimes. And it is a crime! When it comes to human life and our unborn babies, it seems that we take it as our cheapest commodity on earth.

Proof of Life

Fingerprints: Two people cannot have the same fingerprints. So far as forensic science has been able to determine, not even identical twins have prints that are exactly matched. This helps makes the analysis of fingerprints still one of the main means in which to identify people involved in a crime. The fingerprints and D.N.A., of these babies make them a separate life entity and an individual human being with separate, different lives from their mother

I think you already know what God's position on this is, but I will give it to you anyway. It's so simple, even a little child can understand this. This is one of God's Ten Commandments.

Exodus 20:13 NIV: "You shall not murder."

Not enough for you? Try this one.

Luke 17:2 NIV: "It would be better for them to be thrown into the sea with a millstone tied around their neck than to cause one of these little ones to stumble."

Jesus is talking about children, when He says little ones, and that includes our unborn babies.

Will God forgive you of this wretched, despicable act, whether having an abortion done, or in some part involved in that abortion? Let us just hear it from God.

Acts 2:38 NIV: "Peter replied, 'Repent and be baptized, every one of you, in the name of Jesus Christ for the forgiveness of your sins. And you will receive the gift of the Holy Spirit."

1 John 1:9 NIV: "If we confess our sins, He is faithful and just and will forgive us our sins and purify us from all unrighteousness."

Matthew 6:14-15 NIV: "For if you forgive others for their transgressions, your heavenly Father will also forgive you. But if you do not forgive others, then your Father will not forgive your transgressions."

Romans 3:23 NIV: "For all have sinned and fall short of the glory of God."

For all of you ladies thinking about having an abortion—DON'T! If someone is trying to talk you into having an abortion, walk away! If nothing else, put the baby up for adoption. There are many parents out there who would be overjoyed to adopt your newborn child.

If you are considering having an abortion, I have three things to say to you.

1. Don't!
2. Please Do Not!
3. BY THE GRACE OF A HOLY, FORGIVING GOD, PLEASE GIVE THAT BABY LIFE!

The Ten Commandments

Exodus 20:1–17 KJV

Thou shalt have no other gods before Me
Thou shalt not take the name of the LORD thy God in vain
Remember the sabbath day, to keep it holy
Honor thy father and thy mother
Thou shalt not kill.
Thou shalt not commit adultery.
Thou shalt not steal.
Thou shalt not bear false witness against thy neighbor.
Thou shalt not covet thy neighbor's house
Thou shalt not covet thy neighbor's wife

Peace

The meaning of the word "peace" in Webster's dictionary:

1. a state of tranquility or quiet
2. freedom from disquieting or oppressive thoughts or emotions
3. harmony in personal relations
4. a state or period of mutual concord between governments
5. used interjectionally to ask for silence or calm or as a greeting or farewell

Peace, peace, we hear it all the time. Everyone has an idea how to achieve peace. They have peace conferences. There are countries getting together to become united in peace. But where is it? This world gets more violent almost daily, but what can we do? How can we achieve true peace, or is there such a thing? There is a song called, 'Peace In The Valley', but that song is actually about after we die or the rapture and and before "The Great Tribulation," when Jesus comes back and sets His kingdom on earth.

Revelation 21:2-3 NIV: "I saw the Holy City, the new Jerusalem, coming down out of heaven from God, prepared as a bride beautifully dressed for her husband. And I heard a loud voice from the throne saying, 'Look! God's dwelling place is now among the people, and He will dwell with them. They will be His people, and God Himself will be with them and be their God.'"

Of course, there is that Christmas song, "I Heard The Bells On Christmas Day," that says: "Of peace on Earth, good will to men," on the last line of every verse.

Also, in the Bible it says:

Luke 2:14 NIV: "Glory to God in the highest heaven, and on Earth peace to those on whom His favor rests."

But where is this peace everyone keeps talking about and looking forward to? If we look to men, it is not there. But you can have peace, God's Peace, at this day and time? It is there. It may not change the personal problems, situations, or trials you are going through, but it is still there. I personally need a hip and knee transplant, but I still have the peace of God within me. Even when I get out of a chair, or car, and it feels like a sharp knife cutting in me, the peace of God goes with me.

Colossians 3:15 NIV: "Let the peace of Christ rule in your hearts, since as members of one body you were called to peace. And be thankful."

John 14:27 NIV: "Peace I leave with you; my peace I give you. I do not give to you as the world gives. Do not let your hearts be troubled and do not be afraid."

I would love to leave you with these last two scriptures. Seek God and He will give you the peace you seek.

Numbers 6:24-26 NIV: "The LORD bless you and keep you; the LORD make His face shine on you and be gracious to you; the LORD turn His face toward you and give you peace."

I found out by reading the 23rd Psalm (see next page) over and over that it will give you more and more peace. There is power in God's Holy word. Try it. I promise you, it works. How powerful, wonderful and true are those words. Maybe as you read them, you will achieve the real sense of the word "peace". God's peace.

The 23rd Psalm

23rd Psalm 1–6 KJV

The LORD is my shepherd; I shall not want.
He maketh me to lie down in green pastures:
He leadeth me beside the still waters.
He restoreth my soul:
He leadeth me in the paths of righteousness for His name's sake.
Yea, though I walk through the valley of the shadow of death,
I will fear no evil: for Thou art with me;
Thy rod and Thy staff they comfort me.
Thou preparest a table before me in the presence of mine enemies:
Thou anointest my head with oil;
My cup runneth over.
Surely goodness and mercy shall follow me all the days of my life:
and I will dwell in the house of the LORD forever.

Trials And Tribulations

Guess what? No matter who you are, Christian, or not, we all have them. Those dreaded trials and tribulations that come into our lives. Is there anything we can do about them? Are we just destined to have them till we die? The answer to both questions is one big "YES". Some people blame their problems on a curse placed on them, a topic I do not plan to talk about. Others say God does not like them. Not sure what they are doing to think that. Others say it is an act of God. They may be right. God has put His wrath upon this world before.

Genesis 7:17–22 NIV: "For forty days the flood kept coming on the earth, and as the waters increased they lifted the ark high above the earth. The waters rose and increased greatly on the earth, and the ark floated on the surface of the water. They rose greatly on the earth, and all the high mountains under the entire heavens were covered. The waters rose and covered the mountains to a depth of more than fifteen cubits. Every living thing that moved on land perished—birds, livestock, wild animals, all the creatures that swarmed over the earth, and all mankind. Everything on dry land that had the breath of life in its nostrils died."

Genesis 19:13 KJV: (Two angels talking to Lot about destroying Sodom and Gomorrah.) "For we will destroy this place, because the cry of them is waxen great before the face of the LORD; and the LORD hath sent us to destroy it."

And don't forget about that mean old devil. He plays a part in some of the bad things happening. Did you ever think that some of the bad things that happen to us are our own fault. In my case, for example, I used to smoke before becoming a Christian. Now I have Chronic Bronchitis. Just because I became a Christian does not take away what I have done to cause the damage from smoking.

Genesis 6:7 ESV: "Do not be deceived: God is not mocked, for whatever one sows, that will he also reap."

What I sowed was cigarettes, and because of it, I reaped Chronic Bronchitis. So, what does the Bible say about trials and tribulations?

James 1:2 NIV: "Consider it pure joy, my brothers and sisters, whenever you face trials of many kinds."

Romans 12:12 KJV: "Rejoicing in hope; patient in tribulation; continuing instant in prayer."

I have heard pastors say over the years. It will be one of three things. You're either going to go through, are going through, or are coming out of your trials and tribulations. So, not all that is happening to you may be your fault or the fault of what we are doing to this world. Polluting water and air, plus the bombs we set off, and some of the experimenting going on, like chemical warfare. But is there anything we can do? Yes! There are a multitude of things we can do. Such as stop what you are doing if it is something that you know, either long or short term, may hurt your health. Some of the best solutions to trials and tribulations of all kinds are prayer, reading God's word, going to church, seeking fellowship with other believers, who in turn can also pray for you. Best of all, as believers, we know that once this life is all over, we will have eternal life, with no more of those terrible trials and tribulations.

The Electromagnetic Bomb

Well turn off your radios, and televisions, unplug your refrigerator, and get on your walking shoes. Start a fire to keep warm and cook. Go down to the old stream to get water and do what they did when all this technology was not in place. It was told thousands of years ago that we would have all these new types of transportation, appliances, phones, computers, and all the great things we have gotten used to and taken for granted.

Daniel 12:4 NIV: "But you, Daniel, roll up and seal the words of the scroll until the time of the end. Many will go here and there to increase knowledge."

It said "time of the end" and look how we have progressed over the last 100 years. So, the end is so very near. First there was the atomic bomb, which is talked about in scriptures written thousands of years ago in the Bible.

Zechariah 14:12 KJV: "And this shall be the plague wherewith the LORD will smite all the people that have fought against Jerusalem; Their flesh shall consume away while they stand upon their feet, and their eyes shall consume away in their holes, and their tongue shall consume away in their mouth."

This is exactly how an atomic bomb works, but back then they neither had, nor knew of any technology even close to this. If you have doubts about what I am saying, I will let you do the research for yourself. Now, about what I said in the first paragraph. There is a bomb called the Electromagnetic Bomb. I went to the source below with some information on this bomb.

APA Mirror—US Air Force Air & Space Power Journal—Chronicles. High-Power Electromagnetic Pulse generation techniques and High-Power Microwave technology have matured to the point where practical E-bombs (electromagnetic bombs) are becoming technically feasible, with new applications in both strategic and tactical information warfare. The development of conventional E-bomb devices allows their use in non-nuclear confrontations. This paper discusses aspects of the technology base and weapon delivery techniques and proposes a doctrinal foundation for the use of such devices in warhead and bomb applications.

It is, indeed, a frightening scenario—and it isn't the only threat to the nation's electricity grid. U.S. critical infrastructure is also vulnerable to cyber and physical attacks. The risk of such attacks is real and growing.

Please do not get scared and go out and dig a hole to live in. Don't buy tons of food or anything else. From all that I have read, the technology for this is not fully developed yet. It is still early in the game. The possibility of this to happen is still quite uncertain, but there are countries out there that would love to have the capability to send one of these bombs our way. Well, put on your jogging shoes or not, I am definitely not a foreseer of the future. Just somewhat knowledgeable of what is out there and thought you should know about it. Below is a list of what could be affected by this type of bomb.

What equipment is most susceptible to EMP?

Anything that operates on electricity or depends on magnetic fields will be affected by an EMP. The following is a short list of equipment that is likely to malfunction or be damaged by an EMP:

1. Computers and computer equipment
2. Appliances containing microprocessors
3. Automobile electronic ignition
4. Automotive computers and electronics
5. All digital TV equipment.
6. Radio, TV, stereo, and recording equipment containing semiconductors
7. Semiconductor electronics (installed)
8. Semiconductor electronics (not installed)
9. Switching power supplies
10. Cellular phones
11. Cellular phone towers
12. LED and compact fluorescent light bulbs
13. Incandescent light bulbs (requires a much bigger EMP than electronic bulbs)
14. Powerline fuses
15. Power generation electronic controls
16. Powerline distribution equipment and transformers
17. Long distance electric transmission lines (insulators)
18. Generators, but only if their current or voltage limits are exceeded
19. Radio and TV transmitters
20. Microwave communication equipment
21. Radar equipment
22. Electronic telephone equipment
23. Satellites and satellite ground stations
24. Anything with a longwire antenna
25. Photovoltaic solar cells
26. Most electronic sensors
27. TV cameras
28. Microphones
29. Tape recordings

30. Computer disks
31. Flash drives
32. Avionics
33. Electronic flashlights and power failure lights
34. Most electronic factory equipment
35. Batteries connected to equipment
36. Meters

(http://midimagic.sgc-hosting.com/emp.htm)

God Out Devil In

It is true. We take out the Bible, the words in the Bible, Prayer, Ten Commandments. We take the word Merry Christmas and change it to Happy Holidays. Children are not allowed to take Bibles to school and are not allowed to pray at schools and all kinds of crazy stuff. It's maddening! Are we that blind? Don't we see that when we take God out of things, then that mean old devil walks right in with a big, ugly, nasty grin on his face. If some of you do not see this, I know I certainly do. Let us start with schools. Because of taking God out of our schools, we see so much murder, guns, knives, drugs, rape, early pregnancy, giving our young children of God birth control, without the parents even knowing it, mass murder and more. Do I really need to go on? After taking the Ten Commandments out of our government, you now see much more corruption. We worry more about the criminal's rights being protected, than that of the victim. Guilty criminals get much lighter sentences or getting off scot-free for the crime they committed, just because of some small loophole in the law. Let's face it, this world is becoming an insensitive, immoral society, and when they say, "Politically Correct," and it is against what is said in the Bible, then I say they are POLITICALLY WRONG!

Let me tell you a true story. Years ago, I went to court to protest my taxes going up. I guess it was supposed to be a courtroom type setting.

We all set at a long table with a stenographer, a couple other people, and me, being my own defender. With no Bible sitting out, when he swore me in, this is exactly what he said. "Do you swear to tell the truth, the whole truth, and nothing but the truth, so help you?" I said: "I do." I was very confused about that. Was that to make me my own God? No Way! I was very nervous. I still regret that I did not say, "So Help Me God!" I wonder what idiot came up with that idea, and I do mean idiot. In case you were wondering, I lost the case.

Not a day goes by that you do not hear about all kinds of mayhem, mass murders, corruption, wars, rumors of wars. How insane can this get? Every time you think you've seen it all, some new and different bad thing happens. Will things ever get better? With the way the world is going and by what I know of the Bible, I doubt it. Not until Jesus comes back after the Tribulation will things get better. Well, you see where I am going with this. That is why I do not watch the news. Years ago, there was a rock and roll song called Dirty Laundry (Don Henley, *The Eagles*) about how people want to hear about all the bad stuff in our world. I sure wish someone would start up a good news television station for people like me. All this is contrary to the word of God. Let me remind you of the first four Commandments.

Exodus 20:3– 5, 7 NIV:

1. "You shall have no other gods before Me."
2. "You shall not make for yourself an image in the form of anything in heaven above or on the earth beneath or in the waters below."
3. "You shall not bow down to them or worship them; for I, the LORD your God, am a jealous God, punishing the children for the sin of the parents to the third and fourth generation of those who hate Me."
4. "You shall not misuse the name of the LORD your God, for the LORD will not hold anyone guiltless who misuses His name."

Could all the catastrophes of hurricanes, earthquakes, tornadoes, volcano eruptions, and all the devastation in the world be by the hand of God? My dad believed some of the things we are doing, like blowing atomic bombs above, and under the ground could be causing some of this, and maybe he was right to a certain degree. Does this mean God is causing some of the chaos? That I do not know, but I personally believe of all the sins committed in this country, and us *leaving* God out, and *taking* God out of more and more things that closely relate to God and the word of the Bible, most definitely has done harm. Maybe God is not causing these problems but simply pulling His hands of protection away from the United States, which used to be a God fearing, God loving country. Take God out of something, and the devil moves right in. Just check our track record of what all is going in these United States.

Pray seriously for the restoration of our country and help us get back to the Bible. We surely need it.

False Prophets
and Teachers

Yes, folks, they are out there in the millions. There are many religions out there that do not believe in our Bible, Jesus, or anything we Christians believe, and talk about. But beware, there are also thousands out there that try to distort God's word to their liking, and sometimes, by doing that, they believe they can do whatever they want, and they profess that what they do is in God's name, but it is not, and it is most certainly contrary to God's laws. They have preachers who use what we call, "watered-down religion," in order not offend anyone and to keep the attendance and all that money coming in. Some of the big churches out there who are doing that. They drag in millions of dollars. But does God have a view on those changes they are making? Sure, He does. Now, I have given you this scripture before, but feel you need to hear it again to keep it in your mind and heart so as you will not fail.

Deuteronomy 4:2 NIV: "Do not add to what I command you, and do not subtract from it, but keep the commands of the LORD your God that I give you."

Revelations 22:18-19 NIV: "I warn everyone who hears the words of the prophecy of this scroll: If anyone adds anything to them, God will add to that person the plagues described in this scroll. And if anyone takes words away from this scroll of prophecy, God will take away from that person any share in the tree of life and in the Holy City, which are described in this scroll."

God is very serious on this matter and it has not changed. That is why He put it in both the New, and the Old Testaments of the Bible.

But what is a false profit?

Urban Dictionary calls a false profit: "Someone that claims to be more than they actually are. They also want people to follow them because of their inflated self-image and misrepresented self-worth." And they go on to say: "Don't idolize the false prophet for this is surely the path to hell."

Wikipedia defines a false prophet in religion: "In religion, a false prophet is one who falsely claims the gift of prophecy or divine inspiration, or who uses that gift for evil ends. Often, someone who is considered a 'true prophet' by some people is simultaneously considered a 'false prophet' by others, even within the same religion as the 'prophet' in question."

But more importantly, what does the Bible say about false prophets?

Matthew 7:15–16 KJV: "Beware of false prophets, which come to you in sheep's clothing, but inwardly they are ravening wolves. Ye shall know them by their fruits." (In other words by their words, works, and deeds.)

Matthew 24:23-24 KJV: "Then if any man shall say unto you, Lo, here is Christ, or there; believe it not. For there shall arise false Christs, and false prophets, and shall shew great signs and wonders; insomuch that, if it were possible, they shall deceive the very elect."

2 Peter 2:1–3 KJV: "But there were false prophets also among the people, even as there shall be false teachers among you, who privily shall bring in damnable heresies, even denying the Lord that bought them, and bring upon themselves swift destruction. And many shall

follow their pernicious ways; by reason of whom the way of truth shall be evil spoken of. And through covetousness shall they with feigned words make merchandise of you: whose judgment now of a long time lingereth not, and their damnation slumbereth not."

1John 4:1 NIV: "Dear friends, do not believe every spirit, but test the spirits to see whether they are from God, because many false prophets have gone out into the world."

So have you had enough? Do you truly understand what God's Holy Word is telling you? So, let me clarify what is being said and give you ideas on how to watch out for these preachers, and teachers, and hopefully, when you see the truth about them, you will run the other way. They will only hurt you in your spiritual walk with God. First of all, ask God to help you find a good Bible based Church. Second, look to the pastor for guidance, and direction, but never put anyone on this earth on a pedestal. Study the Bible, and if the pastor, teacher, or anyone gives you insight that does not sound quite right, do the research and find out for yourself. There are books out there and plenty of information on the internet that will give you multiple opinions on each topic. Find the one, with the scriptures, that coincides with the Bible. I have talked about this before, if the church has a gay pastor, find another one. Do not get me wrong. I believe, love the person, not what they do, whether it be sexual perversion, or anything else. The Bible is very strong in that, as I have said before, the gay life style is an abomination to God in the Old Testament, and in the New Testament. They both say gays will not enter the Kingdom of Heaven. Now God has in the past forgave many of their sins but instructs them to turn away from what they are doing and gives them redemption. Let me leave you with this last scripture on what I just said. This is about the woman who was caught committing adultery and the towns people were going to stone her. Read before and after the scripture and it will give you the complete picture of what actually happened.

John 8:10–1 NIV: "When Jesus had lifted up Himself, and saw none but the woman, He said unto her, 'Woman, where are those thine accusers? Hath no man condemned thee?' She said, 'No man, Lord.' And Jesus said unto her, 'Neither do I condemn thee: go, and sin no more.'

Reincarnation: Fact Or Fiction

Definition of reincarnation by Webster's Dictionary:

1. the action of reincarnating: the state of being reincarnated
2. rebirth in new bodies or forms of life; especially: a rebirth of a soul in a new human body

You would not believe how many people I have talked to who say they are Christians, but believe in reincarnation. So, let me set the record straight on what God has showed me. Before I ruffle anyone's feathers on this topic, I would like to say I do not believe in it as such. It is just another way for the devil to distract people from the truth and prevent them from being saved. Is there something to it? I believe there is, and I believe God showed me the answer.

Many years ago, I was watching a documentary on this, of how someone in this day, and time said they were reincarnated from a Confederate soldier. Someone got into the archives that most people cannot see. Being so old, they are very delicate. All the information he gave was right. Where he fought, during what time, his rank, number of his unit, all the battles he was involved in, when and how he died, and so much more. Now how would this be possible if reincarnation is not a reality? I actually questioned God on this subject and firmly believe He put the answer in my mind, which He has done to other questions I have had in the past. I really wanted to know His perspective on reincarnation. The answer was so very simple. I have wondered why others have not picked up on it. The same evil spirit that was in that soldier, was in that person in the documentary. He had all the information since that demon was there in the Confederate soldier's mind, and simply gave the information to the person in this time. Another way of deception to make us wonder if what the Bible says is really true. Can I prove this by the Bible? Hopefully, I can to your understanding and satisfaction.

Luke 11:24 NIV: "When an impure spirit comes out of a person, it goes through arid places seeking rest and does not find it. Then it says, 'I will return to the house I left.' When it arrives, it finds the house swept clean and put in order. Then it goes and takes seven other spirits more wicked than itself, and they go in and live there. And the final condition of that person is worse than the first."

Mark 9:25-28 NIV: "When Jesus saw that a crowd was running to the scene, He rebuked the impure spirit. 'You deaf and mute spirit,' He said, 'I command you, come out of him and never enter him again.' The spirit shrieked, convulsed him violently and came out. The boy looked so much like a corpse that many said, 'He's dead.' But Jesus took him by the hand and lifted him to his feet, and he stood up. After Jesus had gone indoors, His disciples asked Him privately, 'Why couldn't we drive it out?'"

Mark 9:29 KJV: (I like this scripture best) "And He said unto them, 'This kind can come forth by nothing, but by prayer and fasting.'

Needless to say, some of these evil spirits can be very mean and very hard to be delivered from. These evil spirits, like Satan will be cast to the 'Lake of Fire', (Hell). Surely not a fun place to be.

2 Peter 2:4 NIV: "For if God did not spare angels when they

sinned, but sent them to hell, putting them in chains of darkness to be held for judgment;"

Revelations 12:7–9 NIV: "Then war broke out in heaven. Michael and his angels fought against the dragon, and the dragon and his angels fought back. But he was not strong enough, and they lost their place in heaven. The great dragon was hurled down—that ancient serpent called the devil, or Satan, who leads the whole world astray. He was hurled to the earth, and his angels with him."

Could these evil spirits that can possess a human being be fallen angels. Maybe, but truly, I do not know. More on this in my chapter on demons and possession of a human soul. I hope you are finding some of these chapters of interest, but also that you come into agreement with what is said.

Demon Possession: Demons Of This World

'Demonic Possession' defined by Wikipedia on the internet:

1. "Demonic possession is believed by some, to be the process by which individuals are possessed by malevolent preternatural beings, commonly referred to as demons or devils."
2. "Descriptions of demonic possessions often include erased memories or personalities, convulsions (i.e. epileptic seizures or 'fits') and fainting as if one were dying."

Am I saying that all people with personality or mental problems (I will explain later why I separated personality from mental) are possessed by a demon? Definitely not. I believe most people with some kind of mental, or physical, problem, is not because of demon possession, but a few of them are. I also believe most of the people who have epileptic seizures are not possessed. For example: some of these people could have had head trauma, or some other type of problem to cause these seizures other than being possessed by a demon. I am definitely not an expert on this, so I will not elaborate any more. One thing, if you think Demon Possession was way back in the early times, just search the Bible.

Now, there was a woman who some psychiatrists say had 39 personalities. Someone also wrote a book and made a movie on this. Now as a Christian, I believe she had only one personality, and 38 demons. Why would I think so? Go back to the Scriptures.

Mark 5:2 NIV: "When Jesus got out of the boat, a man with an impure spirit came from the tombs to meet him. This man lived in the tombs, and no one could bind him anymore, not even with a chain. For he had often been chained hand and foot, but he tore the chains apart and broke the irons on his feet. No one was strong enough to subdue him. Night and day among the tombs and in the hills he would cry out and cut himself with stones. When he saw Jesus from a distance, he ran and fell on his knees in front of Him. He shouted at the top of his voice, 'What do you want with me, Jesus, Son of the Most High God? In God's name don't torture me!' For Jesus had said to him, 'Come out of this man, you impure spirit!' Then Jesus asked him, 'What is your name?' 'My name is Legion,' he replied, 'for we are many.'

Go back to the last chapter and read again: Mark 9:25–28 NIV, and also Mark 9:29 KJV

To my knowledge there are at least ten movies based on actual, terrifying, real-life, cases of demonic possession. I have seen the first two but want to see no more. *The Entity*, and *The Exorcist*.

I have had four incidents with an evil spirit in my life I had to deal with and have heard of others along with people who have talked about it on television. I used to watch ghost hunter documentaries on television, where they show you photos, moving pictures, objects being moved, spirits talking to them. I quit watching them, as I could feel the evilness they are tapping into. Now about one of the two times I was a part of a demonic possession. Christian friends of mine and their son visit me quite often. Their son, very rarely, has these headache spells, which he seems to know ahead of time when they are coming on. Only two times did he have these spells when I was with them. I remembering him saying, "Oh, No!", and then it started. He started throwing up, and had a terrific headache. The first time I stayed around to keep an eye on him while his mom and dad went for a walk. In a few minutes after them leaving he gave me a devilish look and said: "I hate you Lloyd," in a very deep voice that was not his own. Soon after that, he waved both of his arms like that of a baseball referee, and said, "I didn't mean it." of course he didn't, for he, his mom, and dad, are like a very close family to me. When his family came back, I prayed for him, and honestly held back on my prayers, not knowing if what I wanted to pray would make someone mad or worry them. The second time, about a year ago, he and his dad came to visit and later in our visit he said once again: "Oh No!", and the headaches and throwing up started again. This time, I put my arms around him and rebuked this demonic possession 'In The Name Of Jesus.' I talked to his dad on the phone a couple days back and he said there have been no more of these spells.

To back up a bit, the first time I encountered a demon was when I first moved to Nashville. I was going to ministry school then and lived in an apartment complex. A friend of mine told me that cabinet doors were opening and closing in her apartment. Things were falling off the shelves and that one of her young grandchildren was talking to someone over by the furnace but she could not see anyone or anything. She asked me to come over to bless her apartment. I asked the pastor of the ministry school to come over to help me. Although I was new at all this, afterwards I went back to my apartment and blessed it using olive oil. The next day that pastor told me in the middle of the night, his wife was awakened with the urge to go check on her three little boys all in one large bed. It turned out, during the night, that the circular fan next to the bed, fell on the bed, got entangled with the sheets, and caught the bed on fire. Luckily, only one of the boys got a couple of his fingers burnt. Was that God who woke her up with the need to check on her boys and did that devil go to their apartment? I strongly feel it was that devil. I asked the pastor if he went home that night and blessed his apartment. He said he hadn't, but was going to do it right then. There were two other times I had a run in with the devil or one of his imps, but the above two were the most profound. Would I like to get involved with another demon? Definitely not. By the way, the strange things happening in that apartment quit after we blessed it.

My advice to all readers, although I have heard of some Pastors/ people who tell you to say this, or that, to the devil. Do Not! Once again, DO NOT get into conversations with the devil. He is much smarter than you think, and would be a great telemarketer, or door-to-door salesman. If you keep a conversation going with him, I promise, in time, he will win and in turn, you will lose, and I mean lose your eternal soul. I will leave you with this last Scripture that I hope you will always remember on this subject.

John 10:10 KJV: (Jesus speaking.) "The thief cometh not, but for to steal, and to kill, and to destroy: I am come that they might have life, and that they might have it more abundantly."

Hell

You know, they talk about "The Great Tribulation", where Satan will have his seven-year reign on earth. It will be gruesome and horrific times to live in. So many people like to use that four-letter word in their speech: "Go to H——," which I have been told a few times in my life. There is a time and a place that far exceeds the anger of that statement. It is called "HELL," a place that many pastors do not even believe in. It is a literal, real place and if your heart is not right with God, you will live there for eternity. Eternity is void of time and is forever and without end and no more hope of being anyplace else.

Webster's dictionary describes "Hell" as:

1. a nether world in which the dead continue to exist: hades
2. the nether realm of the devil and the demons in which condemned people suffer everlasting punishment—often used in curses
3. a place or state of misery, torment, or wickedness
4. a place or state of turmoil or destruction

Although many like to think and want to believe such a place does not exist, it truly does, and if you do not accept the love, forgiveness, believing in faith that Jesus was born of a virgin and died for our sins.

You will get a firsthand view of it. But better than me speaking, why not find out how the Bible describes it.

Matthew 13:41–42 NIV: "The Son of Man will send out His angels, and they will weed out of His kingdom everything that causes sin and all who do evil. They will throw them into the blazing furnace, where there will be weeping and gnashing of teeth."

Matthew 13:49-50 NIV: "This is how it will be at the end of the age. The angels will come and separate the wicked from the righteous and throw them into the blazing furnace, where there will be weeping and gnashing of teeth."

How does that sound to you so far? But let's not quit there.

Matthew 22:13 NIV: "Then the king told the attendants, 'Tie him hand and foot, and throw him outside, into the darkness, where there will be weeping and gnashing of teeth.'"

Matthew 25:41 NIV: "Then He will say to those on His left: 'Depart from me, you who are cursed, into the eternal fire prepared for the devil and his angels.'"

You will need to read the before, and after, on that one to get the full meaning of what Jesus is saying. But who will go?

2 Thessalonians 1:8–9 NIV: "He will punish those who do not know God and do not obey the gospel of our Lord Jesus. They will be punished with everlasting destruction and shut out from the presence of the Lord and from the glory of His might."

Psalm 9:17 NIV: "The wicked go down to the realm of the dead, all the nations that forget God."

Matthew 25:46 NIV: "Then they will go away to eternal punishment, but the righteous to eternal life."

Revelations 21:8 NIV: "But the cowardly, the unbelieving, the vile, the murderers, the sexually immoral, those who practice magic arts, the idolaters and all liars—they will be consigned to the fiery lake of burning sulfur. This is the second death."

You really need to read before, and after, the scriptures, that I gave you to get the true concept of what God is saying. I believe there is much more written about Hell, than Heaven in the Bible. I think God wants you to know what it really is and understand it is a place you really do not want to be. I will elaborate more on who will not be going to Heaven if they do not turn their life over to Jesus in the chapter Sin.

Seven Year Tribulation

Yes, we Christians call it the "Seven Year Tribulation," and if you are not saved, it is something you will have to go through. Just before the Tribulation, God's people will be, as we call it, "Raptured."

1 Thessalonians 4:16–17 NIV: "For the Lord Himself will come down from heaven, with a loud command, with the voice of the archangel, and with the trumpet call of God, and the dead in Christ will rise first. After that, we, who are still alive and are left will be caught up together with them in the clouds to meet the Lord in the air. And so we will be with the Lord forever."

Well if you missed the Rapture, do not take the mark of the beast which is '666', a mark for man.

WhoIsTheBeast.com says 666 comes from Revelation 13 in the Bible. 666 is a human number that is connected with the mark of the beast. Those who take that mark are condemned to hell, with no way of redemption. The rest of what's to happen should give you goose bumps. Some of the things you will have to go through, these are sufferings you are definitely not going to like.

Revelation 13:11–18 NIV: "Then I saw a second beast, coming out of the earth. It had two horns like a lamb, but it spoke like a dragon. It exercised all the authority of the first beast on its behalf, and made the earth and its inhabitants worship the first beast, whose fatal wound had been healed. And it performed great signs, even causing fire to come down from heaven to the earth in full view of the people. Because of the signs it was given power to perform on behalf of the first beast, it deceived the inhabitants of the earth. It ordered them to set up an image in honor of the beast who was wounded by the sword and yet lived. The second beast was given power to give breath to the image of the first beast, so that the image could speak and cause all who refused to worship the image to be killed. It also forced all people, great and small, rich and poor, free and slave, to receive a mark on their right hands or on their foreheads, so that they could not buy or sell unless they had the mark, which is the name of the beast or the number of its name. This calls for wisdom. Let the person who has insight calculate the number of the beast, for it is the number of a man. That number is 666."

Sounds like these beasts are coming out from everywhere. Does not sound very good so far does it? What do you think will happen if you do not take this cursed mark?

Revelation 20:4 NIV: "I saw thrones on which were seated those who had been given authority to judge. And I saw the souls of those who had been beheaded because of their testimony about Jesus and because of the word of God. They had not worshiped the beast or its image, and had not received its mark on their foreheads or their hands. They came to life, and reigned with Christ a thousand years."

That is a tough way to go for following your beliefs, and something you would not have to go through, if you had received salvation before the Rapture. So, is that everything that we will be going through? Nope.

Mark of the Beast Microchips: 666

I know this section is quite lengthy, but it is a must read for all Christians, and non-Christians alike. The technology is here and has been here for some time now. Believe it and do not get caught in the disbelief that this is all a hoax. It was foretold in the Bible thousands of years ago. The scripture below was given to you before and you really need to read it again: Revelation 13:15–18 NIV

Enroll any Brand of Pet Microchip Lifetime Registration with No Renewal, Transfer, or Update Fees! Our lifetime micro-chip registration will never require any annual fee, renewal fee or fee to update your account. Petkey can host your pet's microchip registration so that it is accessible via the Universal Pet Microchip Lookup Tool. If your pet's current microchip registration provider requires an annual fee, now is the time to register your pet with Petkey and never pay another fee to renew or update your pet's registration. Registering is easy and can be done online, over the phone 866-699-3463, or by mail with any brand or frequency of microchip.

U.S. Military Seeking Implantable Microchips in Soldiers

May 8, 2012
By Alex Newman

The U.S. government is developing implantable sensor microchips for use in American troops, supposedly to monitor their health on the battlefield, the Defense Advanced Research Projects Agency (DARPA) announced earlier this year seeking proposals. But critics of the scheme are speaking out, warning that the new technology could just be a prelude to expanding the use of related devices among the general population—with dangerous implications for freedom and privacy.

According to news reports about the development, DARPA believes that being able to instantly receive updates about any potential medical problems among soldiers would give the U.S. armed forces an advantage over adversaries. Calling the implants "a truly disruptive innovation," the agency said the nanotechnology could revolutionize war—especially because most medical evacuations are a result of illness or disease rather than injuries sustained in battle.

But despite supposedly not being used for tracking purposes, at least initially, privacy experts concerned about the expanding use of such technology are sounding the alarm. "It's always in incremental steps," noted activist Katherine Albrecht, author of the book "Spychips" about the threat of rapidly increasing use of Radio Frequency Identification chips.

According to Albrecht, the use of injectable microchips that do not necessarily track people could eventually lead to calls for systems that do. And while she does not expect the government to ever force Americans to accept the chip at "gunpoint," the gradual process of expanding the whole system should be halted now—before it is too late. Captive audiences like soldiers and prisoners, she told World Net Daily, are merely a stepping stone to broader use.

The proposed DARPA system would work by pumping unimaginably small "nanosensors" into the human body to monitor stress levels, inflammation, diseases, nutrition, and more. In addition to feeding doctors real-time information on the physiological state of individual U.S. troops, DARPA hopes to further develop the technology so that it could actually work to treat the problems from within. The agency expects to begin working on the treatment aspect of the program in late 2012.

"The military runs on the strength of its soldiers, and this latest innovation holds promise to bolster the U.S. armed forces by decreasing preventable illnesses and keeping its men and women at the peak of their health," claimed Kate Knibbs in an article touting the implants for Mobiledia, a technology-focused news outlet that was among the first to break the story.

While the safety of the system remains unclear, the agency is reportedly seeking help from the private sector and academia to develop the biosensors and study their potential applications. If tests show initial success in animal trials, American troops—especially Special

Forces—could be next in line for the implants.

"For military Special Forces the practical realization of implantable nanosensors capable of monitoring multiple indicators of physiological state could be a truly disruptive innovation," DARPA said in its announcement of the scheme. And apparently there are already several government-funded efforts to create such systems—albeit not quite as futuristic—that have been at least somewhat successful.

One of the emerging technologies highlighted in press accounts about the implants is a tiny robotic device being developed at Stanford University that can be injected directly into the human bloodstream. The wirelessly controlled robot—small enough to go through veins—is reportedly able to perform tasks ranging from medical diagnostics to direct drug delivery.

"Such devices could revolutionize medical technology," Stanford electrical engineer Ada Poon, who led the project, was quoted as saying in news reports. "Applications include everything from diagnostics to minimally invasive surgeries." The tiny medical robots, however, are still a work in progress.

Numerous technology commentators expressed alarm over the potential slippery slope involved in rolling out the system. But perhaps senior officials could lead the way to assuage those fears.

"Of course, as Commander-In-Chief, the President of the United States will be the first military man to submit to the new nanochips," wrote Stephen Alexander on the blog Technorati, presumably sarcastically. "As should all the Cabinet leaders and Congressional leaders that are 'next-in-line' for the Presidency of the United States."

In 2010, DARPA was also working on brain implants that would use light pulses to control brain cells and possibly even re-route or re-organize mental activity. While that system, too, was supposed to be for U.S. troops—particularly those who suffer from traumatic brain injuries—analysts warned that the implications of the technology were frightening.

Around the world, hundreds or possibly even thousands of humans have already received implantable microchips for various reasons. Pets and animals across America and much of the developed world have as well. Meanwhile, governments and megabanks are increasingly seeking to phase out paper currency in favor of digital options like the so-called "Mintchip" being developed by the Royal Canadian Mint.

Of course, resistance to these types of controversial schemes is growing, too. But with powerful interests pushing to expand the use of implantable nanotechnology in humans, analysts expect the battle between privacy activists and the establishment to become increasingly fierce in the coming years.

Angels In Our Midst

Are there truly angels out there? Do they really exist? If so, are they just in Heaven now or are there angels on earth as I am writing this? The Old Testament talks about angels. The two I am aware of are the Seraphim, and the Cherubim. If there is a 'IM' on the end of the word, that word is plural. They also mention the Archangel, and Guardian angels. Not really sure if they are part of the first two mentioned. Can they fly? I truly believe so or God would not have given them wings.

Webster's dictionary defines Seraphim as: "the 6-winged angels standing in the presence of God"

In a section of Got Answers online, it describes Cherubim as: "Cherubim/cherubs are angelic beings involved in the worship and praise of God. Angels in the Old Testament Scripture visited men and women on earth. I will mention a few.

Genesis 16:7 NIV: "The angel of the LORD found Hagar near a spring in the desert; it was the spring that is beside the road to Shur."

Genesis 19:1 NIV: "The two angels arrived at Sodom in the evening, and Lot was sitting in the gateway of the city. When he saw them, he got up to meet them, and bowed down with his face to the ground."

Exodus 3:2 NIV: "There the angel of the LORD appeared to him in flames of fire from within a bush. Moses saw that, though the bush was on fire, it did not burn up."

You are probably thinking that was all fine for then, but what about now? How about Mary who bore Jesus?

Luke 1:28-30 NIV: "The angel went to her, and said, 'Greetings, you who are highly favored! The Lord is with you.' But the angel said to her, 'Do not be afraid, Mary; you have found favor with God.'

I know that is still a while back so how about now? Well here goes.

Hebrew 1:13–14 NIV: "To which of the angels did God ever say, 'Sit at my right hand until I make your enemies a footstool for your feet'? Are not all angels ministering spirits sent to serve those who will inherit salvation?"

Now that's us. But going on.

Genesis 28:12 NIV: "He had a dream in which he saw a stairway resting on the earth, with its top reaching to heaven, and the angels of God were ascending, and descending on it."

I know that is Old Testament, but that is still going on now. How do I know?

Hebrew 13:8 NIV: "Jesus Christ is the same yesterday and today and forever."

So, that being truth, you shall never find anything in the Bible that says that Genesis 28:12 has ever changed. But the more we get into this, the better it gets.

Is it possible we may even be talking to an angel, and not even know it?

Hebrews 13:2 NIV: "Do not forget to show hospitality to strangers, for by so doing, some people have shown hospitality to angels without knowing it."

I do not know about you, but I believe what the word of God tells us is true. I will tell you for sure though, there are angels in our midst. I have heard people say, after we die, we will have wings. Personally, I do not think so, and the Bible says nothing about it, but I do know this:

Psalm 8:5-6 N.I.V. "You have made them a little lower than the angels, and crowned them with glory and honor. You made them rulers over the works of your hands; you put everything under their feet."

This is talking about man while on Earth. Now it is a different story when we get to Heaven,

1 Corinthians 6:3 N.I.V. Do you not know that we will judge angels? How much more the things of this life!

Your call. I will tell you for sure though, there are angels in our midst.

I will leave you with a quote from William Shakespeare's play 'Hamlet'.

"There are more things in heaven and earth, Horatio, than are dreamt of in your philosophy."

Heaven

The Nuttall Encyclopedia refers to Heaven as: "In Christian theology the place of the immediate Divine presence, where God manifests Himself without veil, and His saints enjoy that presence and know as they are known."

One of the definitions from the English Oxford Living Dictionary is: "A place regarded in various religions as the abode of God (or the gods) and the angels, and of the good after death, often traditionally depicted as being above the sky."

However you want to put it, there is a Heaven and it will be a wondrous, glorious place, but what does the Bible tell us about it?

Revelations 4:1 NIV: "After this I looked, and there before me was a door standing open in Heaven. And the voice I had first heard speaking to me like a trumpet said, 'Come up here, and I will show you what must take place after this.' At once I was in the Spirit, and there before me was a throne in Heaven with someone sitting on it. And the One who sat there had the appearance of jasper and ruby. A rainbow that shone like an emerald encircled the throne. Surrounding the throne were twenty-four other thrones, and seated on them were twenty-four elders. They were dressed in white and had crowns of gold on their heads. From the throne came flashes of lightning, rumblings and peals of thunder. In front of the throne, seven lamps were blazing. These are the seven spirits of God. Also, in front of the throne there was what looked like a sea of glass, clear as crystal. In the center, around the throne, were four living creatures, and they were covered with eyes, in front and in back."

John 14:2–3 NIV: (Jesus talking.) "In my Father's house are many mansions: if it were not so, I would have told you. I go to prepare a place for you. And if I go and prepare a place for you, I will come back and take you to be with me that you also may be where I am."

Jesus is now sitting on a throne on the right of the Father.

Acts: 2:32–33 KJV: "This Jesus hath God raised up, whereof we all are witnesses. Therefore, being by the right hand of God exalted, and having received of the Father the promise of the Holy Ghost, He hath shed forth this, which ye now see and hear."

After the seven-year Tribulation, which is actually seven years of hell on Earth. Jesus will be coming to earth for His 1000-year reign. Presently, He is in Heaven, with the Father, a place I mentioned above.

Revelations 21:2–3 NIV: "I saw the Holy City, the new Jerusalem, coming down out of heaven from God, prepared as a bride beautifully dressed for her husband. And I heard a loud voice from the throne saying, 'Look! God's dwelling place is now among the people, and He will dwell with them. They will be His people, and God Himself will be with them and be their God.'

Oh, what a glorious day that will be for those who believe

Revelations 21:9–21 NIV: "One of the seven angels who had the seven bowls full of the seven last plagues came and said to me, 'Come, I will show you the bride, the wife of the Lamb.' And he carried me away in the Spirit to a mountain great and high, and showed me the Holy City, Jerusalem, coming down out of heaven from God. It shone with the glory of God, and its brilliance was like that of a very precious jewel, like a jasper, clear as crystal. It had a great, high wall with twelve gates, and with twelve angels at the gates. On the gates were written the names of the twelve tribes of Israel. There were three gates on the east, three on the north, three on the south, and three on the west. The wall of the city had twelve foundations, and on them were the names of the twelve apostles of the Lamb. The angel who talked with me had a measuring rod of gold to measure the city, its gates and its walls. The city was laid out like a square, as long as it was wide. He measured the city with the rod and found it to be 12,000 stadia in length, and as wide and high as it is long. The angel measured the wall using human measurement, and it was 144 cubits thick. The wall was made of jasper, and the city of pure gold, as pure as glass. The foundations of the city walls were decorated with every kind of precious stone. The first foundation was jasper, the second sapphire, the third agate, the fourth emerald, the fifth onyx, the sixth ruby, the seventh chrysolite, the eighth beryl, the ninth topaz, the tenth turquoise, the eleventh jacinth, and the twelfth amethyst. The twelve gates were twelve pearls, each gate made of a single pearl. The great street of the city was of gold, as pure as transparent glass."

I know that was pretty lengthy, but I just wanted you to grasp what I am talking about. Friends of mine and I love to travel and go on a couple cruises a year to see some of God's majesty and splendor. I believe Heaven, the first one I talked about, and the New Jerusalem, will be much more than our mind can comprehend. If we could only imagine how wonderful, and awesome these two places are.

Salvation

Remember what was said and done at the cross?

Psalm 22:18 NIV: "They divide My clothes among them and cast lots for My garment.

Matthew 27:45– 46 NIV: "From noon until three in the afternoon darkness came over all the land. About three in the afternoon Jesus cried out in a loud voice, 'Eli, Eli, lema sabachthani?" ("My God, my God, why have You forsaken Me?")

Matthew 27:50 NIV: "And when Jesus had cried out again in a loud voice, He gave up His spirit."

Jesus Being Raised From the Dead

Matthew 12:40 NIV: "For as Jonah was three days and three nights in the belly of a huge fish, so the Son of Man will be three days and three nights in the heart of the earth."

Jesus took away our sins and there is so much written in both the Old and New Testaments on all the topics I brought forth to you.

1 John 3:5 NIV: "But you know that He appeared so that He might take away our sins. And in Him is no sin."

John 1:29 NIV: "The next day John saw Jesus coming toward him and said, 'Look, the Lamb of God, Who takes away the sin of the world!'"

1 Peter 2:24 NIV: "He Himself bore our sins in His body on the cross, so that we might die to sins and live for righteousness; by His wounds you have been healed."

I will constantly remind you of John 3:16, which says all and definitely means Gentiles too. Next comes the last chapter called "Sinner's Prayer." You will soon know why I felt this chapter was important to the book.

Eternal Life:
It's Not A Game!

Like football, basketball, baseball, and many other sports, there are rules, regulations, and guidelines to follow when playing the games. Team sports have what they call a "Playbook," that tells each player what they are supposed to do, and what is expected of them. We have one too, but we call ours a Bible. In professional, college, and non-professional sports, you have winners, and losers. When you win, you go home with a big grin, a trophy, and possibly some money or prizes, like a Super Bowl Ring, which only a very few have obtained. When you lose, of course, you go home with your tail between your legs so to speak, or maybe mentally beat yourself up for the mistakes you made, or better off, think of better ways to play the game when you are on the field, or on the court the next time. Now you are probably wondering where I am going with this. Seeking eternal life is not a competitive game with God where, if you win, it is eternal life in Heaven, if you lose it is an eternal hell. There are only two teams, so to speak, with God. The sheep, who receive salvation and go to Heaven, or the goats, the lost, who will go to darkness, with gnashing of teeth, fire and brimstone, and all the terrible things you will endure there. I will not give you scripture, explaining all the pitfalls, and I do mean pitfalls, of going to hell and the description thereof since I have already given a brief picture of it in another chapter.

Matthew 25:31–33 KJV: "When the Son of man shall come in His glory, and all the holy angels with Him, then shall He sit upon the throne of His glory: And before Him shall be gathered all nations: and He shall separate them one from another, as a shepherd divideth his sheep from the goats: And He shall set the sheep on His right hand, but the goats on the left.

Now as Jesus being the Shepherd, we, as Christians, would be His sheep. In return, the goats are the ones who are lost, destined to a despicable place called hell.

But it's not too late, as long as you still have breath in your life. As they say: "It's not over till it's over." As silly as that may sound, it is the truth. Some people think they will wait until they are older, or just maybe a little later. You have no guarantee folks. You may die in your sleep, a car crash, and thousands of other scenarios out there that may happen to you.

Recently, I have been emailing with the pastor of a church, about some hot topics in our Christian beliefs. Two of the topics, and the beliefs of this pastor, just blew me away. On abortion, she said we should not change the laws, but people's minds. In theory or on paper it may sound like a good idea, but it will take much more than that. When you read my chapter on abortion, Murder In The First Degree, you will not only find God's perspective on this, but what I know of how these abortions are being done. The second thing she said to me, which startled me coming from someone who is a shepherd of the sheep of God, was that the gay life style and marriages are fine and everything is okay because of being saved by grace. I replied to her email with this passage:

Leviticus 18:22 KJV: "Thou shalt not lie with mankind, as with womankind: it is abomination."

Webster's dictionary describes abomination as:

1. something regarded with disgust or hatred: something abominable
2. extreme disgust and hatred: loathing

If the gay life style is an abomination to God, that sounds pretty serious to me. But that was Old Testament views, maybe God changed His mind in the New Testament.

I CORINTHIANS 6:9 NIV: "Or do you not know that wrongdoers will not inherit the kingdom of God? Do not be deceived: Neither the sexually immoral nor idolaters nor adulterers nor men who have sex with men, nor thieves, nor the greedy, nor drunkards, nor slanderers, nor swindlers will inherit the kingdom of God."

Now as far as the being "saved by grace" comment that she made, using the word grace to condone these actions, you would have to change what God said, and just call him a plain liar.

Revelations 22:18–19 KJV: "For I testify unto every man that heareth the words of the prophecy of this book, If any man shall add unto these things, God shall add unto him the plagues that are written in this book: And if any man shall take away from the words of the book of this prophecy, God shall take away His part out of the book of life, and out of the holy city, and from the things which are written in this book."

Hebrews 11:25 KJV: "Choosing rather to suffer affliction with the people of God, than to enjoy the pleasures of sin for a season."

What is meant when it says "pleasures of sin for a season," is the sins we enjoy against God's word will last just a season of our lives, till we get tired of doing it, die, or best of all, get saved.

I finally asked her, if they were actually teaching these things in the classes she goes to or if she was just that unknowledgeable about what it says in the Bible. I never heard back from her. I hope that she will not

116

only read my book with a heart of understanding along with the Bible and have a true change of heart and not try to change God's word. I really do not want her to go to an eternal hell with such outlandish beliefs and take her congregation with her. So, which is it? Would you rather do what you are doing now for a very, very, short time compared to eternity. Or would you rather live a life of luxury, and splendor, with God. It's a free final choice you will have to make!

Sin

I thought you might need to know what sin is before you read the chapters on salvation, and the sinner's prayers. You can easily go to the last chapter anytime while reading this book or hopefully at the end of this book, to accept Jesus Christ into your life.

Webster's dictionary describes sin as:

1. an offense against religious or moral law
2. an action that is or is felt to be highly reprehensible
3. transgression of the law of God
4. a vitiated state of human nature in which the self is estranged from God

Sin is talked about so much in the Bible that I will touch on a just few of the major scriptures.

1 John 3:4 NIV: "Everyone who sins breaks the law; in fact, sin is lawlessness."

Romans 3:23 NIV: "For all have sinned and fall short of the glory of God."

Romans 6:23 NIV: "For the wages of sin is death, but the gift of God is eternal life in Christ Jesus our Lord."

James 4:17 NIV: "If anyone, then, knows the good they ought to do and doesn't do it, it is sin for them."

Do I really need to go further? What are some kinds of sin God talks about? First of all, there are The Ten Commandments, which are in this book, and some of the others are listed below as taken from http://peacebyjesus.witnesstoday.org/40SinsThatWillSendYouToHell.html

1. **Idolatry**: Is. 45:18; Ex. 20:3 Dt. 5:7; 6:5,14; 17:2-7; 27:15; Acts 21:25; 1 Cor. 5:11; 12:2; 2 Cor. 6:16; 1 Thes. 1:9; 1 Jn. 5:21; Rev. 2:14,20; 9:20

2. **Blasphemy**: Mk. 7:22; Lv. 24:16; 1Ki. 21:10; Mt. 12:31; Acts 26:11; James 2:7

3. **Taking the name of God in vain**: Mk. 7:22; Lv. 24:16; 1Ki. 21:10; Mt. 12:31; Acts 26:11; James 2:7

4. **Profanity**: Lev. 19:12; 21:23; Neh. 13:17-18; Ezek. 23:26; 44:23; Mal. 2:10,11; Eph. 4:29; 1Co. 7:14; 1Tim. 4:7; 6:20;; Heb. 12:16

5. **False teachers**: Dt. 13:6-12; Mt. 23:15; Acts 13:10; 2Cor. 11:13-15

6. **Witchcraft**: Ex. 22:18; Lv. 19:31; 20:6,27; 1Sam. 15:23

7. **Child sacrifice and abortions which we talked about earlier**: Lv. 18:21; 20:2; Dt. 12:31; 18:10

8. **Homosexual relations**: Lv. 18:22; 20:13; Rm. 1:26,27; 1 Tim. 1:10

I am going to let you do the leg work on this one. I went to the site above and I see total agreement of this in what God has said. Go to that site. You will find many, many more. But if all these, and many more will send you to an Eternal Hell, is there a way out? Definitely! Let's see what the Bible says on this. First remember the greatest commandment of all.

Matthew 22:36-37 NIV: "Teacher, which is the greatest

commandment in the Law?" Jesus replied: 'Love the Lord your God with all your heart and with all your soul and with all your mind.'"

This is part of the solution. Plus remember the scripture we talked about that almost everyone knows, whether they are a Christian or not—John 3:16—but please read the verses before and after to get all the true meaning of that verse.

Acts 2:38 NIV: "Peter replied, "Repent and be baptized, every one of you, in the name of Jesus Christ for the forgiveness of your sins. And you will receive the gift of the Holy Spirit."

Acts 16:31 NIV: "They replied, 'Believe in the Lord Jesus, and you will be saved—you and your household.'"

Can someone be saved without being baptized? If at all possible, please get baptized. However, I have been asked by family members to witness to someone who was on their death bed and did not have that chance to be baptized. If they truly believed in what they are saying, doing the sinner's prayer with a firm conviction of Jesus in their heart, I truly believe they made it to Heaven. Do I have any scripture on this? Surely, I do. This scripture talks about the two criminals being crucified with Jesus. One denied Him, and the other wanted His forgiveness and salvation.

Luke 23:39–43 NIV: "One of the criminals who hung there hurled insults at Him: 'Aren't you the Messiah? Save Yourself and us!' But the other criminal rebuked him. 'Don't you fear God,' he said, 'since you are under the same sentence? We are punished justly, for we are getting what our deeds deserve. But this Man has done nothing wrong.' Then he said, 'Jesus, remember me when You come into Your kingdom.' Jesus answered him, 'Truly I tell you, today you will be with Me in paradise.'"

Need I say more? May God Bless All Who Read This!

Salvation

Is it really hard to get saved? Maybe some kind of ritual and living a perfect life? Come to think of it, weren't the Jewish people God's chosen people? So, won't they be the only ones going to Heaven?

Genesis 1:2–3 NIV: "The LORD had said to Abram, 'Go from your country, your people and your father's household to the land I will show you. I will make you into a great nation, and I will bless you; I will make your name great, and you will be a blessing. I will bless those who bless you, and whoever curses you I will curse; and all peoples on earth will be blessed through you.'"

He was talking about the state of Israel and all the Jewish people. They are God's chosen people. Do pray for them, and do not despise them. When I pray for them, I pray for Israel and the Jewish people as many of them do not live in the state of Israel.

Now back to the subject at hand. So, aren't we what the Bible calls "Gentiles," eternally lost? I thought the Jews were God's only chosen people? He did not forget about us even in the Old and New Testaments.

Malachi 1:11 KJV: "For from the rising of the sun even unto the going down of the same my name shall be great among the Gentiles; and in every place incense shall be offered unto My name, and a pure offering: for My name shall be great among the heathen, saith the LORD of hosts."

He even foretold about Jesus coming, dying, and being raised from the dead in many Scriptures in the Old Testament to bring in all people who accept Him as Lord of Lords, and King of Kings, and into the great Plan Of Salvation.

On Jesus being born of a virgin:

Isaiah 7:14 ESV: "Therefore the Lord Himself will give you a sign: The virgin will be with Child and will give birth to a Son, and will call Him Immanuel."

Isaiah 9:6 ESV: "For to us a Child is born, to us a Son is given, and the government will be on His shoulders. And He will be called Wonderful Counselor, Mighty God, Everlasting Father, Prince of Peace."

Jesus suffered and was able to take away our sins:

Isaiah 53:3–9 NIV: "He was despised and rejected by mankind, a man of suffering, and familiar with pain. Like one from whom people hide their faces He was despised, and we held Him in low esteem. Surely He took up our pain and bore our suffering, yet we considered Him punished by God, stricken by Him, and afflicted. But He was pierced for our transgressions, He was crushed for our iniquities; the punishment that brought us peace was on Him, and by His wounds we are healed. We all, like sheep, have gone astray, each of us has turned to our own way; and the LORD has laid on Him the iniquity of us all. He was oppressed and afflicted, yet he did not open His mouth; He was led like a lamb to the slaughter, and as a sheep before its shearers is silent, so He did not open His mouth. By oppression and judgment He was taken away. Yet who of His generation protested? For He was cut off from the land of the living; for the transgression of My people He was punished. He was assigned a grave with the wicked, and with the rich in His death, though He had done no violence, nor was any deceit in His mouth."

Jesus dying on the cross:

Psalm 22:16–18 ESV: "Dogs have surrounded Me; a band of evil men has encircled Me, they have pierced My hands and My feet. I can count all My bones; people stare and gloat over Me. They divide My garments among them and cast lots for My clothing."

Jesus being raised from the dead:

Isaiah 25: 8–9 NIV: "He will swallow up death forever. The Sovereign LORD will wipe away the tears from all faces; He will remove His people's disgrace from all the earth. The LORD has spoken. In that day they will say, 'Surely this is our God; we trusted in Him, and He saved us. This is the LORD, we trusted in Him; let us rejoice and be glad in His salvation.'"

But does the New Testament agree with the writings of the Old Testament? Read on and find out. Let us see if the New Testament agrees with that of the Old Testament on the topics we previously talked about:

Jesus being born of a virgin:

Luke 1:30 NIV: "But the angel said to her, 'Do not be afraid, Mary; you have found favor with God. You will conceive and give birth to a Son, and you are to call Him Jesus. He will be great and will be called the Son of the Most High. The Lord God will give Him the throne of His father David, and He will reign over Jacob's descendants forever; His kingdom will never end.' 'How will this be,' Mary asked the angel, 'since I am a virgin?' The angel answered, 'The Holy Spirit will come on you, and the power of the Most High will overshadow you. So the Holy One to be born will be called the Son of God.'"

Matthew 1:21 NIV: "She will give birth to a Son, and you are to give Him the name Jesus, because He will save His people from their sins."

Jesus suffering, dying, being mocked, and gambling for His clothes:

Luke 22:63 NIV: "The men who were guarding Jesus began mocking and beating Him. They blindfolded Him and demanded, 'Prophesy! Who hit you?' And they said many other insulting things to Him."

John 19:16–18 NIV: "Finally Pilate handed Him over to them to be crucified. So the soldiers took charge of Jesus. Carrying His own cross, He went out to the place of the Skull (which in Aramaic is called Golgotha). There they crucified Him, and with Him two others—one on each side and Jesus in the middle. Pilate had a notice prepared and fastened to the cross. It read: 'Jesus of Nazareth, the King of the Jews.'"

John 19:23—24 NIV: "When the soldiers crucified Jesus, they took His clothes, dividing them into four shares, one for each of them, with the undergarment remaining. This garment was seamless, woven in one piece from top to bottom. 'Let's not tear it,' they said to one another. 'Let's decide by lot who will get it.' This happened that the scripture might be fulfilled that said, 'They divided My clothes among them and cast lots for My garment.' So this is what the soldiers did.'"

Sinner's Prayer

I have actually given you two sinner's prayers to help guide you in what you may want to say to God. Why two? Because this is the one most important step you will make in your life.

Prayer One

Dear Father in Heaven.

I come to You with a humble heart, asking forgiveness for all of my sins. I know, by Thy word, that I was born, and will die a sin-ner, but through Jesus Christ only, who died on the cross, and You raised from the dead, bore my sins that I can be saved. I believe You are the true and only living God. I stand firmly, that I believe in the life of Jesus, as told in your Holy Word. I now ask that You wipe my sins away, as if I have never done them. I also ask, for You to send the Holy Spirit to dwell within me. For all this I am eternally grateful. As I send my love up to You my Lord, I ask that You send Your love down upon me, my life, and all that I do. May I be your faithful servant to follow You, lead others to You, and do all that is requested of me, and all that You will guide me to do. In Jesus most Holy Precious Name I pray.

Amen

Prayer Two

Dear precious Heavenly Father.
I come to You in the name of my Lord, and Savior, Jesus
Christ, to ask You to forgive me of all of my sins, cleanse me from
all unrighteousness. I know that my soul is as black as coal, and
that I am a sinner, and have fallen from Your grace and mercy.
Please cleanse me of all my sins and make them white as snow.
I know that Jesus was born of a virgin, and died on a cross, so a
sinner like me might be saved. Please redeem me from this wicked,
and evil world. Please guide me, in my daily walk. Let me be a
light to others, and understand Thy word, so as I may lead others
to their salvation. I know the time is very, very short before Jesus
comes back at the Rapture and I have so much to learn and do.
May I always remember to pray to You and never forget to thank
You for all the blessings You have bestowed upon me. I know I do
not deserve Your forgiveness, nor by any means have I earned it. By
Your grace, and mercy, I know You have heard my prayers and all
my sins are forgiven and there is a place, even for me, in Heaven.
Also, by Your grace I am forgiven, by Your precious blood I have a
new eternal life with You and by Your love, I have an eternal home
waiting for me in Heaven.
Amen

After saying The Sinner's Prayer, or one of your own. If you use it,
you may add or take away whatever you want to make it appropriate
for you. After you say it, what does scripture say?

Luke 15:10 NIV: "In the same way, I tell you, there is rejoicing in
the presence of the angels of God over one sinner who repents."

I too, rejoice in your salvation. Find yourself a good Bible based
church, stay in prayer, read the Bible, keep the faith, and most of all
enjoy your new life as a new creature in Jesus Christ.

2 Corinthians 5:17 KJV: "Therefore if any man be in Christ, he is a new creature: old things are passed away; behold, all things are become new."

Remember, when talking to God, pray deeply from your heart, and with love. However insignificant you think it is or you may think it is to a Most Holy God, God never sees it that way. Always cherish and honor the moments you had in prayer with Him. May God Bless You Always In Your Prayer Life!

Faith, Prayer and Fasting

Faith—you hear Christians and preachers talk about it and in combination with that, they throw in the word "prayer," and sometimes talk about fasting. What are they really? How do they work? All these words can be difficult to talk about, especially when you try to combine them. This will be a difficult task for me, but I will give it my best.

Wester's dictionary defines faith as:

1. belief in, trust in, and loyalty to God
2. belief in the traditional doctrines of a religion
3. firm belief in something for which there is no proof

Does this sound a little confusing, let's see what the Bible says on the same topic.

Hebrews 11:1 KJV: "Now faith is the substance of things hoped for, the evidence of things not seen.

Definition of the word prayer by Webster's dictionary:

1. an address (such as a petition) to God or a god in word or thought
2. the act or practice of praying to God or a god, kneeling in prayer
3. a religious service consisting chiefly of prayers
4. something prayed for

Mark 11:22–24 NIV: "Have faith in God," Jesus answered. "Truly I tell you, if anyone says to this mountain, 'Go, throw yourself into the sea,' and does not doubt in their heart but believes that what they say will happen, it will be done for them. Therefore I tell you, whatever you ask for in prayer, believe that you have received it, and it will be yours."

The Free Dictionary by Farlex describes fasting as:

1. abstinence—act or practice of refraining from indulging an appetite
2. the act of restricting your food intake (or your intake of particular foods)

Matthew 17:20–21 NIV: He replied, "Because you have so little faith. Truly I tell you, if you have faith as small as a mustard seed, you can say to this mountain, 'Move from here to there,' and it will move. Nothing will be impossible for you. But this kind does not go out except by prayer and fasting."

Have I got you even more confused? Hope not. Now, please remember, you do not always have to fast to have your prayers answered, but for the most extreme cases of a more serious nature, it definitely would not hurt. Now let's see if we got this right. Faith is believing something will happen without actually being able to see it at that point. Prayer is a way of not only talking to God, praising Him, or asking for something that you want, or need to happen, and fasting is going without food for a certain amount of time. I particularly would not recommend going on a forty day fast like Jesus did in the Bible. I have heard of people fasting for three days, some going with a specific item they love for a longer period of time, and I even heard of a lady, who just went without her evening meal, so her son could be healed. I heard it took over a year for God to answer that one, but He healed him. God's decisions on what prayers to be answered and when they will be answered sometimes take time.

As a Christian, God will fulfill your needs.

Webster's dictionary describes a need as:

1. a lack of something requisite, desirable, or useful
2. a condition requiring supply or relief
3. lack of the means of subsistence

Philippians 4:19 NIV: "And my God will meet all your needs according to the riches of His glory in Christ Jesus."

But what about our wants?

Dicionary.com describes a want as:

1. to feel a need or a desire for; wish for;
2. to wish, need, crave, demand, or desire;
3. to be without or be deficient in.

Now God does not give us all of our wants. Why is that you ask? Think of all the silly things we have asked for. And if that was so, every child in the world would have a pony. God knows what we need. Not only that, at times, He will bless us with some of our wants.

Now let me get to the depth of all three words. I will give you some of the major scriptures on each topic, and hopefully be able to tie it all in to your full understanding.

First is the topic faith. Remember, we have already touched on the topic of faith with scripture. But there is still a lot more in this wonderful book we call the Bible.

Ephesians 2:8 NIV: "For it is by grace you have been saved, through faith—and this is not from yourselves, it is the gift of God."

1 Corinthians 16:13 NIV: "Be on your guard; stand firm in the faith; be courageous; be strong."

Ephesians 6:16 NIV: "In addition to all this, take up the shield of faith, with which you can extinguish all the flaming arrows of the evil one." (The evil one, of course, is the devil.)

Matthew 17:20–21 NIV: "He replied, 'Because you have so little faith. Truly I tell you, if you have faith as small as a mustard seed, you can say to this mountain, 'Move from here to there,' and it will move. Nothing will be impossible for you. But this kind does not go out except by prayer and fasting."

2 Corinthians 5:6–7 NIV: "Therefore we are always confident and know that as long as we are at home in the body we are away from the Lord. For we live by faith, not by sight."

Second, we have been talking prayer.

Psalm 34:15 NIV: "The eyes of the LORD are on the righteous, and His ears are attentive to their cry."

1 John 5:14 NIV: "This is the confidence we have in approaching God: that if we ask anything according to His will, He hears us."

James 5:16 KJV: "Confess your faults one to another, and pray one for another, that ye may be healed. The effectual fervent prayer of a righteous man availeth much."

But how do we pray?

2 Chronicles 7:14 NIV: "If My people, which are called by My name, shall humble themselves, and pray, and seek My face, and turn from their wicked ways; then will I hear from heaven, and will forgive their sin, and will heal their land."

Matthew 6:5–8 NIV: (Jesus talking.) "And when you pray, do not be like the hypocrites, for they love to pray standing in the synagogues and on the street corners to be seen by others. Truly I tell you, they have received their reward in full. But when you pray, go into your room, close the door and pray to your Father, who is unseen. Then your Father, who sees what is done in secret, will reward you. And when you pray, do not keep on babbling like pagans, for they think they will be heard because of their many words. Do not be like them, for your Father knows what you need before you ask Him."

Then Jesus gives us an example in Matthew 6:9–15, called "The

131

Lord's Prayer," which is in this book.

And thirdly, fasting.

Matthew 6:16–18 NIV: "When you fast, do not look somber as the hypocrites do, for they disfigure their faces to show others they are fasting. Truly I tell you, they have received their reward in full. But when you fast, put oil on your head and wash your face, so that it will not be obvious to others that you are fasting, but only to your Father, Who is unseen; and your Father, Who sees what is done in secret, will reward you."

I think that is a very good scripture on how you should fast. Please note, if you want any more scriptures on any of these three topics, the Bible is full of them, and I truly believe, it will be fun for you to do more research on your own. Now, to tie all this up. First, through faith, and prayer we know God will hear our prayer. Call out in the name of Jesus, as He is our Advocate to the Father in Heaven. If possible, sometimes it is good to pray on bended knees. There is no limit to where, and when, you can pray. When praying, it is best first to tell God how much you love Him, and if you want, even sing to Him. Next, you should always pray for others, such as family, friends, fellow Christians in church, our leaders, our country, problems you may hear about on the news, and of course, the list goes on. Next to last, pray for your needs, and maybe even wants, and finally end off with words of love, thanks, and how grateful you really are to our Heavenly God. First thing in the morning when I get up and the last words out of my mouth before going to bed, I say. "I love you, Jesus."

Prayer

For those times when you are having trouble finding the words to say, you may use or modify the following prayer to suit your needs. This is a prayer I said to God recently, after starting this book when it seemed like everything was coming down on me and was against me and the more I did for God, the bigger and heavier my cross seemed to get.

Dear precious, precious, Heavenly Father.
come to You in the name of my Lord, and Savior, Jesus Christ.
I love You with all my heart, soul, mind, and being, but so many
times I fall short of being the Christian I feel You would want me
to be. Please help me when I stumble, redirect me when I follow
the wrong path, hold me when I am hurting, listen when I need
a close friend to talk to, speak to me as I try to listen, give me full
understanding when I read Thy Holy Scripture, but most of all,
know that You are the most important part of my life. Sometimes
the words I speak seem so futile, actions, and deeds without merit,
words meaningless, and the snares of the evil one surround me.
Please always guide me, help me, forgive me, love me, especially at
times I feel unloved, even though I am not worthy of Your love, or
forgiveness. Please watch over me, and never let me far from Thy

sight. May I always stay humble in Your presence. My love for You is true, and deep down in my heart. Always, your faithful and loving servant, now and forever.
Amen!

Make note, that The Lord's Prayer, which is in this book on the next page, is the best guide on how to pray, but I hope this one may help a little in what to say. Please remember though, God is only a prayer away.

The Lord's Prayer

Matthew 6:9–13 KJV

Our Father which art in heaven,
Hallowed be Thy name.
Thy kingdom come,
Thy will be done in earth,
as it is in heaven.
Give us this day our daily bread.
And forgive us our debts,
as we forgive our debtors.
And lead us not into temptation,
but deliver us from evil:
For thine is the kingdom,
and the power,
and the glory,
forever.
Amen.